Adventures and Challenges: Real Life Stories by Girls and Young Women

**Frances A. Karnes
and
Suzanne M. Bean**

Gifted Psychology Press, Inc.

GPP

Adventures and Challenges: Real Life Stories by Girls and Young Women

Cover Design: ATG Productions, Inc.
Interior Design: Spring Winnette

Published by
Gifted Psychology Press, Inc.
P.O. Box 5057
Scottsdale, AZ 85261

Printed and Bound in the United States of America

04 03 02 01 00 5 4 3 2 1

Library of Congress Cataloging-in-Publication Data

Adventures and challenges : real life stories by girls and young women /
[edited by] Frances A. Karnes and Suzanne M. Bean.
   p. cm.
  Includes bibliographical references (p.).
  Summary: Stories of women who pursued their quests for adventure and exemplified positive risk taking in both mental and physical domains. Includes resources to
assist in planning an adventure.
  ISBN 0-910707-35-9
1. Young women--Biography--Juvenile literature. 2. Girls--Biography--Juvenile literature. 3. Women adventurers--Biography--Juvenile literature. 4. Adventure and
adventurers--Case studies--Juvenile literature. [1. Women--Biography. 2. Adventure
and adventurers.] I. Karnes, Frances A. II. Bean, Suzanne M., 1957-

HQ1229 .A27 2000
305.242'092'273--dc21
[B]   99-053241

ISBN 0-910707-35-9

Table of Contents

This book is dedicated to Mary Ryan Karnes and Cameron Meriweather Bean, both of whom have already had several adventures. They know that girls and young women can achieve difficult goals, and we wish them well in all the adventures still to come.

Acknowledgments

Many people assisted with the preparation of this book. Hundreds of individuals were contacted in our search for adventuresome girls and young women. With their support our endeavors have come to fruition. To those girls and young women who wrote about their adventures and worked with us to complete this volume, we admire you for all your many accomplishments and thank you for allowing us to share your stories with the world.

We continue to have productive careers in nurturing collegiate environments at The University of Southern Mississippi and Mississippi University for Women. Students, staff, faculty, and administrators have given encouragement for which we are deeply grateful. We extend special gratitude to Lane Sample at Mississippi University for Women and to Carolyn Foil at The University of Southern Mississippi for their constructive feedback on the book as it progressed.

The talented staff at The Center for Gifted Studies at The University of Southern Mississippi has offered ideas and given technical assistance. Heather Ratliff typed the manuscript; Kristen Stephens gave input to several aspects of the book; Barbara VanDuser supervised the many programs conducted by the Center. We appreciate all of their endeavors.

Our families have always been supportive of our many writing projects; their enthusiasm for our work regarding girls and young women continues over the years. To our husbands, M.

Ray Karnes and Mark Bean, we wish to acknowledge much love and understanding. To John, Leighanne, and Mary Ryan Karnes and to Meriweather and Hudson Bean, thank you for all you do for us and please keep your sense of adventure about all aspects of your lives. To Christopher Karnes, your love of life and special guidance will always be with us as an influence.

To Gifted Psychology Press, our publisher, we extend a special note of appreciation for making this book a reality. Your understanding of the needs of girls and young women is appreciated.

Introduction

Current research tells us that girls and young women need positive role models if they are to develop a strong self-concept and high self-esteem, and to achieve self-actualization. Girls have been given greater opportunities to participate in organized physical activities in the schools since 1972 with the passage of Title IX. We know that girls who participate in physical activities are far less likely to use drugs and significantly more likely to attend college. Yet very little has been written about girls and young women who have used their physical and mental abilities to be adventurers.

Included in this book are stories of girls and young women who have pursued their quests for adventure and exemplified positive risk taking in both the mental and physical domains. Section One: *Girls' Stories* highlights girls who have been involved in various adventures within our country and abroad. One young woman from the South took a five week freighter trip to South America. As the one and only passenger, she has many exciting on-board and port-of-call adventures to share. In a jungle adventure, a young female primate scientist describes the physical and psychological aspects of establishing the camp in the bush, as well as the dangers and joys of studying the behavioral patterns of lemurs. A young woman returning for the second time to the Arctic inspires all of us with her amazing story of adapting to the environment, problem solving, and physical endurance.

At the end of each story, the reader is introduced to the personal side of the girls and young women: from age, hometown and hobbies, to educational level and family information, through short biographies. Most of the girls' stories tell how they became interested in a specific area of adventure, preparation necessary to participate, obstacles along the way, persons who assisted them, physical preparation, and aspirations and goals for future adventures. These girls and young women offer inspiration, advice, and encouragement to you to engage in your own adventures.

Section Two: *Planning Your Own Adventures and Challenges* focuses on what it takes to be an adventurer and how to get started. Discussion of the benefits of adventures may encourage you to try a new experience. Guidelines are provided to help you analyze your individual strengths and interests before you consider various types of adventures. Strategies are given for each of the following elements: risk taking, goal setting, physical preparation, mental preparation, logical precautions, and perseverance for dealing with obstacles.

Section Three: *What Others Have Said and Accomplished* offers quotes and inspirational statements on several dimensions of adventure. A timeline is provided to highlight the accomplishments of girls and young women in history in many areas of human endeavor. For those interested in specific adventures, a listing of how-to books is provided in section three. Also provided are books on females who have been involved in adventures and biographies focusing on famous adventurers. The majority of books listed are written for youth and young adults.

We hope this book gives you the inspiration to pursue positive adventures throughout your lifetime. Think about those you can begin now, those you may wish to pursue in the next few years, and those you'll save for later in your life. Enjoy your quest for adventures and challenges!

Section I

Girls' Stories:
Adventures
in the United States

My Trip
Climbing and Rappelling

*A mountain climb and rappelling trip
showed Rachel that even walking
off a cliff can be rewarding.*

by Rachel Harris

One Tuesday we stood frozen in awe, looking up at the massive rock we were about to climb. Our group consisted of 13 sixth graders, accompanied by two adult leaders and one eighth grade leader. We were half of the sixth grade at The College School, located in St. Louis, Missouri. Every year, each class went on a special camp-out. This year our class did "The Wilderness Experience." For the trip, we spent five days and four nights in the "Wilderness" at Shawnee National Forest in Illinois. There were no bathrooms, no showers (and, boy, did we stink), no tents...and none of the useful things we take for granted. While we encountered many challenges and adventures on this exciting trip, none was as incredible as this one.

After our first night out, we were all pretty well rested. When we got to the cliff, we were told it would be 100 vertical feet on the route we were to climb up, and 120 feet down on the

3

route we would take coming back. The rock looked frightening, although we had all climbed it before. We tried hard to prepare for this rock by climbing smaller rocks and by climbing fake rocks such as the ones in our gym. Despite our practice, nothing could have fully prepared us for this challenge.

One of the two routes up was called "Camel's Back," named for the odd shape of the rock that looked like the bump on a camel's back. The other route was called "The Crack," because of the large crack running up the rock face. I climbed that one.

The beginning was not very hard, but once I got about 40 feet up, the challenge started. The crack became wide enough to get my foot (or even my whole leg in some spots) stuck. The climb in those parts was straight up! There were hardly any foot or hand holds suitable to use, let alone to reach. To top that, another challenge struck us in the face—literally! There were thousands of bugs flying around madly. They looked like orange ladybugs, but were much worse. They stung us and squirted out orange sticky juice. They would stop at almost nothing to drive us insane. I tried to ignore the little pests, but needless to say, I couldn't.

Finally, with a lot of encouragement and support from below, I made it past the worst of the climb. I'm not quite sure how I did it, or just where I stepped, but I made it. The rest was pretty much downhill from there. Well, not really downhill, but it was a lot easier. Nothing could actually be quite as much downhill, or should I say 'downcliff,' as what I did after that on my way down.

There were two ways to get down from the top. One was to walk down a boring, long path. The other way was to rappel. I, and most of my classmates, chose the rappelling. Our harnesses were hooked on securely and fastened to an adult and a few large trees at the top. I was the one to choose how fast I would go down. I was the one holding the end of the rope. I was the one with the pressure. And, needless to say, I was very nervous.

At the beginning, we had to step over the edge of a cliff, which was one of the hardest things I have ever done. I bet not many people have walked over the edge of a cliff backwards! But I, and most of my classmates, can say proudly that we have. My courage came from my teacher and friends at the top, as well as my friends at the bottom. My teacher encouraged me by reassuring me that I would be fine and that the ropes would support me all the way. Sure enough, he was right. I took a breath, and stepped over the cliff.

Once I was down a bit, I started going faster and faster. My fright had ceased until I hit the edge of a long flat part on which I was "walking." Or rather it was the fact that I didn't hit the rock that bothered me. My friends instructed me to stay calm and just jump away from the rock wall as I went down, and sure enough, it worked. I started building up speed again, and I soon reached the bottom. I sent my equipment back up for the next person to use and finally ended my most exciting adventure ever.

Looking back at that experience, it was great. However, I never would have imagined it, or that it could be so fun, without my school. For one thing, I never would have known about how to do this, or anything about it. I also wouldn't have had the courage to do such risky things without the support from my friends and teachers. I learned a lot from my experience. One thing I learned was that I can do almost anything I attempt. I almost gave up when I hit the tough part while climbing, but I stuck to it and made it to the top. I learned that by trying and trying, when you hit a troublesome place, you eventually succeed, and are rewarded. In this case, the reward of climbing was the spectacular view from the top and the exhilarating feeling of accomplishment.

If I had the chance, I would most certainly do this experience again partly because I loved it so much, but also because I would like to do better. I would try a new path up next time or try to beat my old time. I would not be as scared going down. I would help and encourage people as much as they helped me, or even more. I would have the time of my life all over again.

My advice to other young adventurers is to be careful. Far

too many accidents happen when people fool around without knowing what they are doing. Always wear the proper equipment and clothes when climbing, including helmets and harnesses. Use good and sturdy equipment, too, like ropes. And the most important key to successful adventures is to remember to have fun!

Rachel Harris

Rachel Catherine Harris was born June 21, 1987, at Barnes Hospital in St. Louis. She is the first child of Peggy and Larry Harris. She and her younger brother, Peter, have lived in the same house on Washington Avenue all their lives. Rachel started at The College School of Webster Groves in first grade and now is a sixth grader there. She enjoys school and is currently taking a special advanced math course, which she likes. An avid reader and writer, Rachel had her first poem published in the St. Louis Post-Dispatch *newspaper when she was five years old. The paper also published one of her stories when she started third grade. She has been active in Girl Scouts since kindergarten. Rachel recently started speed skating and hopes to win a medal at her first competition.*

The Squeeze

On an adventure trip, a small endeavor leads
to life-long memories for Bevin.

by Bevin Kloepper

As I stand there in the breath of the night air
and take off my sweatshirt, my heart jumps with
excitement as I get ready to enter The Squeeze.
In the dim light of the moon I see a tall rocky
wall reaching for the sky. The main path goes off
to the right into the dark silent night, but a mys-
terious dark line creeps up the face of the rock
straight ahead. As the group waits in whispered
voices, I wonder what adventures lie ahead....

I am on the Wilderness Experience. It is a trip that the
College School sixth-graders take every year. We go out in the
wilderness for five days where we are met with the challenges of
hiking, canoeing, problem solving, rock-climbing, and most of
all, teamwork. It's not an easy week either. We have no bathrooms, electricity, and no roof over our heads. We also have to
hike with big backpacks that carry all our gear for the week. If
your pack falls in the water or gets left out in the rain, it's wet for
the week. We also have to hike from morning to night, pack just

7

two pairs of underwear (because everything weighs something), and sleep by ourselves for one whole night. However, it's probably one of the greatest experiences I've ever had and if I get a chance to go again I will. We got to rappel off a 100-foot cliff, eat a dinner of soft tacos and smooshed cookies at one o'clock in the morning, and eat lunch in a canoe. Like one of my friends said, "The wilderness dirties our bodies but cleanses our souls."

It was the first night of our Wilderness Experience. We had driven three hours from school to get to the wilderness. Dusk had fallen and night was settling in as we reached the mysterious dark crack in the side of the cliff. "Mrs. P," the school director and one of my leaders, announced that this crack is called The Squeeze. When she said this, everybody started to talk about how their sisters or brothers had told them about it or how excited we were. My friend Kate and I jumped up and down and talked to each other at the same time. We didn't understand what the other was saying, but we pretended that we did. Next, Kevin, our other leader, tapped us on the head, telling us to get in line. As we stood in a line I could only see the silhouette of people because part of our adventure was to go without flashlights. I was in between two boys named Andrew and Basil. Mrs. P and Kevin told us that our adventure would be to slide through the crack in the rock. Any little thing in our pockets, even our thick sweatshirts, could stop us from getting through the tight squeeze. Mrs. P and Graham (the junior leader) went in first, followed by the rest of the group. The adventure began as we started to move.

My mind was cluttered with thoughts of both excitements and worries. As I entered the small opening, I had to turn my body sideways so I could fit between the cold smooth rocks. As my hands touched the walls of the rock all my worries went away and I only thought of the moment. My feet inched along the rough uneven ground that was littered with rocks and wet leaves. I chattered with Andrew, Basil, and Kate, who were closest to me in the line. We were in a single file line because the crack was so narrow that even our smallest sixth-grader could not stand facing forward to go through. It got darker and darker and smaller and smaller in the crack until I could not see my hand in front of my face, not that there was enough room to move it. The crack in the rock was so tight it seemed like it squeezed out all the light.

From the front of the line news was passed back that the hard spot was coming up. I thought immediately that I would make it, no matter what, and if I had to pry myself through I would. I was determined. I thought about this until I got to the hard spot. I was determined, I thought once more. Then I pushed up with my right hand on Basil's shoulder behind me, sucked in my stomach, lifted my foot up the two-and-a-half foot rock and pulled myself up. I had made it! In my mind, I rejoiced. I knew the rest of The Squeeze wouldn't be as hard.

I made sure Basil was okay, and then I slid up the rest of The Squeeze, where I was met by the moonlight and a hand to help me up. On top of the rock there was a lot of excitement and talking. After most of us got out, Mrs. P took us one at a time to see the rock we had just climbed. It is about 75 feet high. I peered at the leaves and sweatshirts down below, and couldn't believe I had made it.

It took a lot of teamwork, belief in myself, and determination to succeed in an adventure like this. I learned I have to trust other people, and to enjoy every moment because it might only happen once. I also learned I should relax and go for it because if I don't, I might not get another chance.

When everyone was finished, Mrs. P and Graham took us down a path that led back to where our adventure with The Squeeze had started. As I walked back to the vans in the darkness with the wind hitting my face, I thought that although this adventure of squeezing through cold cramped rocks sometimes no wider than seven inches apart may have been small compared to other adventures during the Wilderness Experience, I will always remember it. I will remember that all adventures count, even the small ones, because they all teach me lessons. That night in my sleeping bag I wrote it all down so I would never forget it. The memories are mine forever.

Bevin Kloepper

Bevin Kloepper is 12 years old and was born on January 23, 1987. She lives in Chesterfield, Missouri, with a four-year-old sister, Tessa, and a thirteen-year-old brother, Kyle. She has two kittens named Onyx and Gandalf and a full-sized collie named Jake. Bevin enjoys climbing (especially trees), swimming, and playing basketball. She attends The College School of Webster Groves. Right now her favorite electives are field hockey, volleyball, and 3D art. In her spare time she enjoys writing, reading realistic fiction, and, of course, socializing. Bevin also likes exploring the woods behind her house and playing with her little sister.

Rock-Climbing Adventures

Sarah's goals and determination lead her
to enjoy adventure and the wilderness.

by Sarah Rondot

October 26th was a bright and sunny day. I was leaving on a school wilderness trip. This particular trip was going to be five days of hiking, backpacking, canoeing, hiking, and–did I mention hiking? We were all packed and ready for five days of backpacking in the wilderness. My school, The College School of Webster Groves, is an adventurous school, you might say. We go on a lot of trips and do a lot of hands-on activities. We have many exciting, thrilling, attitude-building adventures. Most of these adventures start out to be fun, but end up frustrating.

"It's going to be five days of pure torture," I thought as I boarded one of our school vans. I mumbled and slumped in my seat preparing for a long, boring ride. By having a bad attitude, I started the trip off on the wrong foot. Feeling morose and discouraged, we finally arrived at our destination–a bluff that was supposed to be our campsite for the night. Being as late as it was, I uncrumpled my sleeping bag and drifted off to sleep feeling sad and helpless.

Day Two–my adventure now began. This was the exciting part. This is not another one of those essays on how an adventure changes someone's life! Well, maybe it is. Read on.

The second day of our trip, a climb on McKanda Bluff was planned. We piled into the vans and rode off. McKanda Bluff is more than a 100 foot climb straight up. We all saddled into harnesses and made our way up. In many parts it was frustrating, but almost everyone made it up to the top. I sat and looked out, gazing at the dry climb. Trees lined the outside of the trail to the climb and I wandered along their edge. I thought to myself "I am never going to be able to climb that thing...ever!!"

The climb looked scary, yet exciting. I would have rather (at the time) skipped it altogether, but I was also looking forward to it. It felt weird to be feeling two different things at the same time. Yet it felt right. It was soon going to be my turn to go.

Jagged rocks stuck out and made it look impossible as I creaked my neck all the way back to see the top. I watched other sixth graders climb silently and swiftly move their bodies along the rock surface, as if they were daddy longs legs silently reaching and pulling up the cliff. My palms started to sweat and I looked up as the sun beat down on my tightening muscles.

"Sarah, are you ready?" my friend screams to me. "Yeah, SURE," I think, "My turn!" My harness tightened and my trace eight dressed, set, with knot secured, I step up to the powerful, huge rock engulfing me. I could have just heard the rock talking to me, saying "If you touch me roughly, I'll throw you off; so beware!!" But I could also hear the soft, gentle side of the rock saying "You are a beginner; I will be gentle, but please, be careful."

The first few steps were easy. "Anywhere you can put your knee, you can put your foot, and climbers say life is too short to spend on your knees." I remembered my teacher's words. I struggled up the rock, a few feet higher. I stopped, then climbed a little more so I was now almost half way up.

I pushed myself up and stood straight and tall. I looked around and took in the high altitude air. I looked across the land

and saw pine trees as far as the eye could see. The trail wound through them, all the way to a far off dirt road.

"All right," I thought, "this may not be as bad as I thought it would be." Now here came the hard part. The rock became more vertical and harder to climb and I clung to my surroundings uneasily. A rising sensation boiled in my stomach. Fear? Excitement? Adventure? I started to cry for one of those reasons—I'm not sure which. My legs wobbled and my fingers shook as I moved slowly upward.

At one point, I was so scared that I froze up and just clung there for a long time. My mind was racing and finally I persuaded myself to continue. So I went on. As I looked around at the possible things I could do in this predicament I made a goal, no matter what, to make it at least four feet higher than where I was "frozen."

It took awhile just to take one step. At the time, my heart was saying, "Keep on going! You can do it!" But my body was saying, "Stop! You're pushing too hard!"

Along the way, I had to plan out, problem solve and wisely maneuver my body along the rock. Easy enough, someone else might think. Yeah, right. I finally persuaded myself to do it, and I took a dreadful climb up; one step then another. Another. And...finally! I made it! I was there! Tears of happiness at my success streamed down my face as I smiled to myself and sighed a sigh of relief.

I pictured all those female rock-climbers, climbing for the first time, and it inspired me. My attitude changed and I loved and succeeded in everything I did the rest of the trip.

At the end of the week-long wilderness expedition, I sat down on the hard, wet ground, hugging my knees to my chest. We were all then distributed out in the wilderness, by ourselves for about two hours. We were sent out to write in our journals and reflect on the trip. I spent my time thinking.

I buried my face in my oversized coat that smelled like the rain from the night before, the musty smell of being in a Zip-Loc bag for too long, and the smoky smell of the campfire. Now it probably would have smelled bad. But then, it was familiar. I looked around not wanting to leave the adventurous wilderness. "I'll probably be back," I thought. "No! I will be back; I'm positive I will!" I thought about how much I learned and the people who helped me through it all. I thought about all my friends who were there when I needed them, and my family for preparing me for adventures that usually only privileged kids would experience. I think back on how I've learned to respect myself and keep on trying. I think I've really figured out who I am, what I am, and who my true friends are.

"If I could do it all over again," I think to myself, silently crying tears of joy and pain, "I would do it in a heartbeat, but I would definitely do it with a better attitude." I figure with a good sense of adventure and an open and humble attitude, I can accomplish anything!

Sarah Rondot

Sarah Rondot didn't think she was an adventurous soul until going rock climbing and discovering her love of adventure. Sarah is 12 years old and lives in St. Louis, Missouri. She has one brother away at college and her parents are divorced. Sarah lives with her mom but sees her dad often. She loves sports, especially soccer, and now after her experience, rock-climbing. She also enjoys writing and carries a journal with her whenever possible. She is on her sixth year of piano and is becoming a very good pianist. Für Elise was the last piece she played.

Sarah loves to take risks and to solve problems. Whether it's climbing a 100-foot bluff or playing a difficult piece on the piano, Sarah tries to push herself that extra little step.

My Mountain Adventure

A primitive trip on horseback takes Jade back in time with her parents.

By Jade Ashley

I am Jade Ashley and I am 11 years old. I am going to tell you a story about an adventure I took with my parents when I was six years old. I will tell it as best I can remember.

My story begins when my family and I started planning and packing for a horse trip out West in the Uintas Mountain Range in Utah and Wyoming. We were going to ride and camp with other families for several days and nights and end at the American Mountain Men National Rendezvous. (A rendezvous is a kind of meeting where you meet up with other people; it's pronounced RON-day-voo.)

We would spend several days of primitive camping there. We would do the horse ride in primitive clothing and with primitive camping gear. When I tell you we used primitive things, I mean that all our clothing and gear was just like stuff that was used before 1840. The horse gear was primitive too; my mom and I used Indian squaw saddles with nicely decorated bladder bags to carry our jerky and trail food. I didn't get hungry while riding because I could eat food from the bladder bag on my saddle pommel all day long.

15

Everybody who does this kind of camping has a story about who they were for that time period in history. On the trip they dress and act as if they were this historical person. My dad dressed as a mountain man with Indian leggings because he married an Indian woman (mom) and they had a child (me). My mom and I each dressed Indian or Native American because my real history also includes Shawnee Indian ancestry.

Mom and I wore dresses even though it was hard to ride horses without the padding that pants give you. Our dresses were made with lots of ribbon trim like the Shawnee women made their dresses. We also wore necklaces made of beads to be pretty and wore our hair long and pulled back just like Shawnee women did. We wore center-seam leather moccasins that mom and dad made and mom decorated with wool and beads.

Shawnee women didn't wear hats, but for the horse trip that year we wore hats trimmed with ribbon. I did not know that I was the only child riding on this trip with 17 other grownups. I also didn't know until later that some of the adults were worried that I might not be able to handle this trip. They didn't know my parents had taken me primitive camping since I was two years old and that I rode trail with dad and mom on our farm in Ohio.

Mom laughs about the first time I went to a rendezvous. I wore moccasins and a breech clout around my waist and, because it kept falling loose, people called me Miss Moccasins. Mom and I have Indian names. Mom is Makwa Tamsah (Bear Woman) and I am Winter Star. I can sign my name in Indian Sign Language. Dad's name is Snake (Kanapaqua). At rendezvous, the men practice sign language because sometimes the tribes didn't speak the same language and the mountain men had to use sign language to communicate with them. The following is my memory of this adventure with mom and dad:

We were finally saddled and riding away from Brownie Lake, Utah. It was our first day. I was riding a rented horse named Sargent. My mom rode a mare named Jody and dad rode a horse named Bud. We also had a pack horse to carry all the gear. The trail went up and down and it was windy and cool for the end of June.

On day two, we were in the Ashley Forest. We saw a lot of beaver ponds. The beavers didn't hide from us. They kept chewing on wood and swimming. I was led by my dad on a lead rope attached to my horse (which I did not like but dad said he didn't want the rented horse to run away with me). We rode through high meadows and it was still windy. My mom and I both got mountain sickness with bad headaches. In the evening my dad awakened me from a nap and led me out to a clearing. There we saw big moose that thought our horses were other moose. Once they saw us, they trotted away. I went exploring in the meadow after that.

On day three, it was windy with sunshine. We had oats for breakfast. We rode through rugged country that day. We also saw lots of antelope. We rode through thick stands of lodgepole pine to get to our campsite. It was hard to get our horses and gear through them because the trees were so close together. We also rode through marshy beaver ponds. It was a long ride to look for water. I went exploring that day and found a log to play on. That night it rained. In the middle of the night, we were awakened by water running through our lodge. We were wet and cold. Dad started a fire with flint and steel to warm us and dry out our gear.

The next morning, one of the other women riders, Samantha, helped me saddle my horse. She always offered to help me get ready for the trail each day. Samantha lives in Montana and really knows how to ride a horse.

On day four we had ridden through sagebrush which had a real nice smell. I fell asleep on my horse, and we rode all day long. We rode along the Uintas Mountain Range of Utah and Wyoming. It was cold, and we were heading into the wind, but I was still strong.

On day five we rode across Henry's Fork of the Green River. On the other side of the stream was the American Mountain Man Rendezvous. The other people were waiting to greet us. Everybody was dressed in clothes that were the kind people wore before 1840. Now we would camp for a few days here and I would look for a new friend before we traveled back home to our farm in Ohio.

I went on this adventure with my parents because they wanted me to and because I thought it would be fun to ride horses in the West. I was prepared to go with my parents on this adventure because I have been on horses since I was two years old with my dad. I have also done primitive camping with my parents since I was two years old. I get courage to ride horses from my dad because he loves horses and we have always owned horses.

From this experience, I learned how people from that time in history had to dress, live, and eat. The food wasn't always what I wanted to eat, but I ate it anyway. It is definitely more difficult to wear dresses on a horse than to wear pants like I normally do. My dad was the leader for our family telling mom and me what we needed to do, but we all worked together. My dad, mom, and Samantha helped me on this trip. My female role models were mom and Samantha. Mom always got me dressed properly and made sure I ate, but Samantha helped me saddle my horse while dad was loading the pack horse with camping gear.

My advice to others would be try something new before deciding to hate it. I didn't know if the trip would turn out good or not, but it turned out to be a fun adventure and I was on the cover of the *Mountain Man Magazine!*

Jade Ashley

Jade Camille Ashley was born in Portsmouth, Ohio, on December 26, 1985. Her parents are Bruce Marion Ashley and Sharon Copas Ashley. Jade has long brown hair and green eyes. She is 5 foot 2 inches tall and 11 years old. Jade lives on a farm with her parents. She has two brothers and one sister from her father's prior marriage. Her siblings no longer live at home; however, Jade fondly recalls playing "Legos" and "He-Man" with her big brother Jason when she was three years old.

Jade is a physical person. She loves horses, archery, canoeing, basketball, softball, cheerleading, and volleyball. She also plays flute and piano. Her favorite activity is riding horses. Jade won First Place in the State of Ohio in long distance competitive trail riding in her first year at this sport. Since the time of writing this, Jade has won First Place Junior in the subsequent two years, entitling her to retire and keep the trophy. The family farm has eight horses, three cats, four snakes (Dad's), one iguana (Jade's), one dog (Coco), and ten cows. Jade's competitive trail horse is an Arabian named Khemo Shalom. Khemo is thirteen years old.

Jade is in the sixth grade this year, and she likes art, band, math, and social studies. A good student with excellent grades, Jade has also been nominated for Citizenship of the Month Award at school and was voted President of Student Council. Jade is a Girl Scout; and along with her troop, she walked in the local American Heart Association Heart Walk to raise money for prevention of heart disease. Jade is vibrant and energetic; she has a smile for everyone. It is clear to all that she expects to have an exciting life!

19

Conquering the Chaos

*When Lesley found out she could help
other kids read, she ran with the idea.*

By Lesley Weinstein

I sat in a Barnes and Noble bookstore holding some over-
ly glorified hot beverage and staring across the table at a
friend, but my mind wasn't anywhere near there. I was looking through the United Way service catalog for a volunteer
job. Almost all the organizations required a person to be sixteen and over or eighteen and over. The ones that didn't
weren't interesting or satisfying, although stuffing envelopes
would give me one wonderful sense of accomplishment. I sat
wondering why it should be so hard to help, why age should
limit ability, and why even when I was able to do something,
it meant nothing to me.

These thoughts continued as I stood at the starting line of a
road race a few days later. Then mid-race it hit me–why not
start something myself? I decided that whatever I did would
only be open to anyone eighteen or under, but it wasn't until a
few days later that I saw the true value of my decision. I thought
about how kids would not feel intimidated, would not have to
live up to anyone's standards but their own, and would not feel
outdone by adults. This would be something that *they* could do.

When I got home I e-mailed a teacher, asking if I could drop an elective during the upcoming trimester and pursue an original endeavor during that time. A few e-mail notes later, I somehow got myself committed to managing a massive "project"–a run for kids to help kids. I had three months to start with nothing and end up with everything–a run called "Kids-4-Kids."

Acquiring a Missouri Runner magazine, I e-mailed the editor for advice. His first response back was something like, "Since there isn't enough time to write a book on this subject, here's what you need to know." Now I started wondering what I had gotten myself into, but I knew that it was too late to back out. Someone once said, "Leaders walk the talk." This would have to be my motto for the next twelve weeks.

A few days later, I was on the phone with my friend, Graham, and I asked him what I should do. My first thought was for the run to benefit kids with cancer or kids that had been abused. However, if I turned any profit at all, it wouldn't mean much because these were huge organizations with millionaire donors. Second to that, the degree of their problems was something I had never endured, so it would be like another random service project–going through the motions but not feeling anything. Then, Graham's mom, Kathy, got on the phone and opened a new door. Why not benefit America Reads, national literacy program that she directs in St. Louis? A literacy program was perfect. Kathy was a personal contact and appreciative of a small monetary donation. Most of all, I liked the idea. Who doesn't have a favorite story? I felt that kids could relate to this organization–an organization that helps all kids learn to read by third grade so they can read to learn throughout the rest of their lives. If you ask kids, most of them remember their favorite books as a kid and can tell you their favorite books now. Being read to as a child, I felt there were probably more kids touched by reading than kids who were touched by abuse or serious illness like cancer.

Einstein once said, "Great Spirits have always encountered violent opposition from mediocre minds." I learned he was right just a few weeks into pursuing my adventure. Almost immediately I was told by various people that I should push the date of the run back, that I couldn't make it happen by the date I had planned. I wasn't prepared for those comments. I asked myself why they said things like that; why they didn't seem to understand that I had made a commitment. If I were an adult, they probably wouldn't have made those comments. It didn't seem fair that I was setting a serious goal and not being taken seriously. I learned that this wasn't about what I could do for them or for myself, but what I could do for the program that the run was benefiting. I went ahead with the original plan.

I didn't have the benefit of knowing what to do, how to plan it, the chain of events, or who to go to. I was hit with a tidal wave of anxiety. I started with trying to get a course, permits, and a location. People gave me a hard time because I was only four-teen years old, yet I persisted. Through trial and error I gathered sponsors. I designed a T-shirt and flyers, and through friends I got deals on printing. I went to *Runner's World* magazine for race numbers and a running store called Fleet Feet for a time clock. Slowly the run was piecing together, but I had one of my biggest obstacles yet to come–getting my peers interested.

I guess when most of them heard the word "run," they immediately flashed back to those hot sweaty days in physical education when we ran the mile; those runs were not very enjoy-able. Next, the thought of getting up early on a Sunday morning was just as devastating. I had never thought about what would happen if they weren't interested in signing up. It seemed like nothing I said or did made a difference. Begging, bribing, and everything in between didn't alter the numbers of participants; I had hit a wall, but thankfully not a ceiling. I just decided to let things run their course, that whatever happened would happen for a reason, and now I'm glad I trusted that intuition.

My adventure peaked on the race day when 103 kids showed up to run in a 5K or one mile race. They all laughed together, ran together, and unknowingly raised $1,500. Afterwards we all found a spot in the grass and had an awards ceremony. Smiles were constant as some of them realized that they could help if they tried, and it didn't have to be conventional. At least that's what I learned. I also learned to stick up for myself and for what I thought was right because I was the only one who knew what I was capable of. Before the Kids-4-Kids run I never took much notice of the "You can do it if you really try" types of speeches–but now I know what they're all about.

Without the help of some wonderful role models, I wouldn't have been able to accomplish my task. My principal, Jan Phillips, my mom, Kathy Becherer, and Judy Weng and Sarah Webster were all amazing women who played instrumental roles in helping me throughout those crazy three months. They, as well as the rest of my teachers, friends, family, and especially Andrew Hume, displayed great interest, tolerance, understanding, and cooperation. They also took impressive risks for my benefit.

Not only would I do it again, but I plan on doing it again. It was worth it to get there on race day and see so many kids show up to help each other and themselves. All the work, all the frustration, and all the self-doubt were worth even just a minute of a day like that.

I don't feel comfortable giving advice to others about being an adventurer because I don't see myself as an amazing adventurer in the first place. All I know is that you should live up to your own standards, not anyone else's. Don't accept anything less than the most you can give, because eventually it will just become a habit and you'll end up doing some great things. I think you'll find, like I did, that insanity is worth the adventure.

Lesley Weinstein

Lesley carries on a relatively crazy life in St. Louis, Missouri. She was born on September 18, 1984. She has a sixteen-year-old brother named Scott; her mom is a homemaker and her dad is a sales representative. Lesley lives in a suburban community called Kirkwood where she has spent her whole life so far. Lesley is most comfortable outdoors, preferably in the middle of nowhere, living out of an overstuffed Kelty pack. Her friend, Graham, taught her most of this. She is aiming for NOLS (National Outdoor Leadership School) for next summer and enjoys climbing, swimming, and running. If you asked her to pick three words to describe herself, she would most likely reply with sarcastic, leader, and persistent–all of which tie in somehow with her adventurous traits.

Climbing Mt. Whitney

Lora hailed a storm to reach her peak goal.

By Lora E. A. Wilbur

I love to hike. Hiking is a magical way to explore, challenge and test yourself. So when our Girl Scout leader, Mrs. Sharon Allemann, announced that our summer trip would be a fifty mile backpacking trek in the Sierra Nevada Mountains, culminating at the top of Mt. Whitney (elevation 14,495 ft.), I was thrilled. As the months slid by I slipped from confident to apprehensive. Could I make it? What if someone got hurt? I had so many questions.

Finally the day came and I was leaving on possibly the biggest adventure of my life. Our group consisted of fourteen girls, three boys and nine adults. We drove to Cottonwood Lakes campground near Lone Pine, California. The mountain air was cold and sharp and we soon bundled up in warm clothes. As I set up my tent it struck me; I was *here*–there was no turning back!!

The first day's hike was short; but for me it was hard. Getting acclimated to the 9,000 foot elevation while carrying fifty pounds is never easy; and the first day is always the hardest.

That night we camped at Chicken Springs Lake. From there we hiked to Rock Creek Lake, a long but mostly flat trail. At Rock Creek Lake we had a layover day and our first rainstorm. My tent

27

stayed dry but some of the others in my group were not so lucky.

The next day we resumed hiking. The first four miles were nicely graded and almost flat with lots of water crossings. The last mile was uphill at a 60 degree angle; but when I reached the campsite it was worth it. Gyotte Creek was a rocky creek surrounded by patches of grass. We ate our lunch sitting on rocks in the creek. I took pictures of everyone sitting on the rocks relaxing.

By mid-afternoon the sky was dark with rain clouds. We raced through dinner trying to beat the weather but the storm hit us just as we finished. It was a light rain so we tried to sit out and sing but it was no good. There were too many bugs. I finally gave up and went to bed early.

The next day we headed out for Crabtree Meadows, a long five miles. Crabtree Meadows had our first Ranger station. The Ranger made us camp in two separate groups. After dinner my group went down to visit the other half of our group. We were energetic that night and entertained ourselves by singing and learning a Spanish song and dance from Trinidad. That night I stayed up late to sing and watch the stars. The sky in the mountains is gorgeous; you could see so many stars that they melded together into creamy swirls.

The next day, August 6th, was a day to remember; I woke up with butterflies. It was the day before *THE DAY*–the day that would take me to the peak of Mt. Whitney, I hoped. Mrs. Allemann had told us we would not be able to hike to the summit if it rained. We took our time packing this day; it was only a three mile hike to our next campsite, and we had all day.

Finally, we were all packed. To start the hike we had to cross a creek. I had crossed it the day before with no trouble but the water had risen during the night and the logs were slippery. Most of the group had crossed before me so I was not worried. But as I stepped forward on the logs I suddenly found myself sitting in rushing water up to my chin! I was so astonished that I could not move until one of my friends yelled, "Your camera is floating downstream!" I made a futile grab for it, then pulled myself up. A friend was standing at the edge of the creek to help me out of the water. As I stood there, shaking in the cool air, water pouring off of me, I was unsure whether to laugh or cry. Laughing being the easier way out, I laughed hysterically. I changed my socks but had to hike in wet clothes and boots. An easy three miles became difficult to the point of impossibility.

Finally, I made it. Collapsing onto a rock, I looked up, and up, and up at the monumental granite face of Mt. Whitney. It was awesome. It was frightening. We went to bed early that night so we could get up at 4:30 a.m. the next morning to prepare for the climb.

Getting up the next morning, I didn't have time to wonder what I had gotten myself into. We hit the trail at 6:30 a.m. It was going to be all uphill. As I hiked up past Guitar Lake, the trail became deeply rutted with a stream running down the middle. By the time I reached Lower Hitchcock Lakes, the water was gone but my boots were soaked once again. I hiked on, up the steep, rocky trail.

The trail wound on endlessly, short switchbacks giving way to long ones. As I climbed higher, I found myself looking down on Hitchcock Lakes. While my friends and I discussed the lake's unusual name, we heard a rumble and the mountain range opposite us seemed to shake. It was an avalanche. Properly shaken, we continued but spoke only in whispers for a long time. The rocky trail was in the shade and snow still clung to the cold rocks in sheltered places.

I reached the junction (called trail crest) a little after 11:00 a.m. The three miles had felt like six, and although the thin air was not bothering me, one of my friends had to go slowly. As I dropped my pack on the rocks and covered it with a trash bag, I realized that I was only two miles from the peak of Mt. Whitney. I was going to make it!

I pulled on my day pack and started up the trail. I hiked swiftly, but carefully. The trail was strewn with rocks, some knee high. The trail wound around the mountain and suddenly I could see the peak with its stone building and lightning rods. The final path to the peak was steep and the trail virtually disappeared. I picked my way slowly between huge flat rocks and suddenly I was there!

As I signed the register, a piece of hail rolled off the hut's tin roof and slapped me on the cheek. I was too excited to worry. I made my way over to where the rest of my group was eating lunch. I dropped my pack and stepped onto the highest rock there.

The view was gorgeous–with lower mountains behind me and flat desert in front. I could see the city of Lone Pine in the distance. I was on the highest point in the contiguous United States. I was on top of Mt. Whitney! As I sat down to eat my lunch it started to hail. I took shelter in the stone hut's tiny room with others in my group. It was so crowded everyone was standing.

It stopped hailing after a while, and most of the people left, but a few of us stayed. As we were getting ready to leave, Dayton Allemann opened the door and told us we needed to leave; the storm was getting worse and there was lightning in the distance.

We threw on our packs and hurried down the mountain as carefully as we could because the stones were slippery. As we hiked, it started to hail again. Rounding a curve in the trail, I came across some of my group huddled in an alcove in the rock wall, waiting out the storm. The hail started coming down harder and faster then, mixed with snow, and the lightning and thunder crashes were getting closer. To keep ourselves calm we sang any song we could think of from *Amazing Grace* to *Take Me Out To The Ball Game.*

After a good half hour passed, the storm let up slightly and we joined hands and made our way slowly down over snow-coated rocks. As we came in view of the trail crest, a cheer went up from the others waiting there. We started singing our troop song. I dusted snow pellets off my backpack and pulled it on. It was after 3:00 p.m. and there were still three miles of Trail 99 switchbacks left to hike that day.

I still do not know how I got down those switchbacks. I was so tired I almost fell asleep on the trail several times. Finally I reached the camp. I went to bed right after dinner. I was tired! Never has a sleeping bag on a rock felt so good!

Two days later we hiked the rest of the way down to the end of the trail. As I sorted through Whitney T-shirts in the Whitney Portals store, it struck me. I had not only peaked Mt. Whitney but I had done it in a hail storm! I had reached my goal. I had done it!

Lora E. A. Wilbur

Lora Wilbur, age 15, lives in Stanton, California, with her parents, two younger brothers, and three younger sisters. She enjoys hiking, bicycling, music, frogs, and spending time with her friends. Lora is a sophomore at Asian Academy Christian Home School and is an active member of Senior Girl Scout Troop 1241 and BSA Explorer Post 1962. She is an experienced backpacker and has 182 hiking miles. This is her tenth year of Girl Scouting.

Last year Lora earned Girl Scouting's Silver Award and is now working toward her Gold Award. She plans to attend Long Beach State College and earn her Ph.D. in Physical Therapy.

When asked about backpacking Lora says, "It's hard, and at times it seems impossible, but when you look back on it, the good memories always outweigh the bad."

Adventures in Field Ecology

In Michelle's many adventures, which include whitewater rafting and body surfing, she learns to accept challenges and adapt to her surroundings.

By Michelle Marincel

The silence of the woods penetrated me, sinking deeper through my skin. The refreshing peacefulness of the Smoky Mountains in the distance felt like home–like I had lived there all my life. A gentle breath of wind rustled autumn leaves struggling to hold on.

Tree,
Tall, silent, strong and free,
Fills me with loving glee,
Slender branches reach to see,
Always watching over me
Tree.

It was a relief to be in the calming woods after the long van ride. Ten hours of driving in one day with the same classmates gets tiring.

The purpose of this trip was to learn more about field ecology, which is a trimester long science course at our school. Our

33

trip that semester took us to many different places–to the Smoky Mountains, Nantahala River, Okefenokee Swamp, and Sapelo Island. I set up my tent that first night with my two close friends, Rachel and Kyrstin.

We were to hike up to Laurel Falls in the quiet of the night. The twinkling stars seemed to wink at me as I steadily hiked up the path. Everything was peaceful and tranquil except for the clomp of my boots on the path. Whirling wind whipped through my hair as I stole glances at the promising stars through the leaves, although just to the left the earth stretched out far below. We saw the falls.

*The thunder of water echoes through my head as the music of
nature comes into view. Flashlights dot the falls as the
laughing waters hurry downstream
leaving me with only memories.*

*The stars twinkle as they wink at me,
seeming to promise many
special moments like this. As the icy wind whips
through my hair
and rustles the trees, I feel like I'm in my own magical world.*

*Sadly, I say my good-byes, and taking one last peek, I try to
memorize the beauty of Laurel Falls. I will never forget these
dancing waters as their music fades away
like a beautiful dream.*

Quietly, as I began the downward hike after this exhilarating experience, I walked away from everyone else so I could feel the power of the forest. With my flashlight low, I controlled the clomping of my hiking boots as I tuned in to the true sounds of nature. The chorus of frogs echoed in my ears amid the thunder of water still rushing through my head.

With stars peeking through the reddened leaves and the fresh smell of plants touched with dew, I felt the true meaning of the mountains. I felt a part of them.

34

Finally back at our campsite, I eagerly lay down. The cool night air nipped my exposed skin as I hurriedly snuggled my tired body into my cozy sleeping bag. It was a relief to rest after this long and exciting day.

The next day I gulped water frequently as I trudged up seven hundred feet in two miles. The rocky trail made the going tough but I promised myself I *would* make it to the top of the Chimney Tops.

"Get it!" I screamed. The tiny salamander slid through my fingers as I grabbed for it, leaving me clutching a handful of moss. "There it is!" I announced excitedly as I motioned for Trevor to capture it. Pigmy salamanders are only about an inch and a half long. Trevor caught it so we could look at it, then he let it go.

I pushed myself further and higher, until I took my last upward step to the top. Radiant sun rays fingering through the clean air reached me and filled me with a feeling of accomplishment. I reached my arms high in the air, feeling as if I could touch the sky.

Free
The word now seems real. All worries left behind,
seven hundred feet below. The wind seems to be inviting me,
inviting me to come along and become part of it–
to fly from
mountain to mountain, to be on top of the world, to be free.
The sun beats down on my back, as stubborn as the
mountain itself. It seems to send its messenger rays to
penetrate my skin, sucking all the moisture out of me.
Although shady spots are scarce, it is worth the energy
to find one.

The mountain is a challenge, a challenge that takes trust
in myself and in my friends to help me up to the next rock
and for me to do the same for them.
Sometimes a false step might mean my life, or a slip would
surely endanger my classmates.

35

*We are there for each other to conquer this
mountain together, and the rewards are breathlessly fulfilling.*

I walked freely down Chimney Tops, stopping occasionally at one of the many streams to try to catch another salamander in the icy cold, fast flowing mountain water. One salamander found me crawling in the freezing water through a small tunnel under the path. We chased each other from one end to the other. What a thrill!

Later that evening I took a hike with my class up to Clingman's Dome. This dome is the highest point in the Smokies and is located on the Tennessee/North Carolina border. The cold wind whipped through my hair and clothes, as if trying to rip them from my shivering body. The cold of the evening was unforgiving, but the tranquil, brilliant hues of the sunset made up for it.

The land stretches far into the horizon. The delicate view of the Smokies seems like a promise–a promise of good weather and a promise of memorable times as we pursue our last outdoor trip together. The glowing sun melts into the horizon. Its fingering rays reach up past Clingman's Dome, up beyond the clouds, up into space, into the appearing stars.

Tired, I made my way down the mountain and reached the van just as the last hints of pink and orange faded away behind the horizon.

More driving was necessary; this time we traveled to a new destination–Nantanala Outdoor Center–where I would stay in a cabin and where we would later be doing some whitewater river rafting.

This was a whole new experience. My raft tore through the swirling, threatening waters as we plunged our way down rapid after rapid. We hit the corners of rocks, paddling together to spin around in circles off of them. We soon dubbed this procedure the "washing machine." White water rafting was such a thrilling experience, all so new and exciting to me.

Splash! I jumped out of our raft, helped pull it to shore, and went to scout out Nantahala Falls. After almost four long hours of hard paddling, the muscles in my hands and arms cried out to me. In spite of blisters, I was not stopping. My four raft partners and I, along with our eighteen classmates, scrambled down the gravel path with cool water streaming down our legs. I tried to run, but the bulkiness of my life jacket and my paddle weighed me down. We were headed for a viewpoint where we could "scout" or check out the next rapids we were about to paddle. We all came to a halt as we watched, fascinated, as other rafters and kayakers risked the threatening falls. The route looked scary, with water roaring over boulders below the falls. I couldn't wait for our chance at it.

I crowded around my teacher with the others as Tim explained more safety rules. He told us to paddle harder the more we felt like we were about to fall out or tip over. He said if for some reason we were swept out into the swirling waters, he would throw a rope; we were to grab the rope and throw our arm over our shoulder, and immediately kick our feet up to the surface to keep from being pulled under by the current or snags.

Anxiously, I watched for the first group to come into view as I hung over the bridge's rail. The current swept them down the rapids and over the falls. Perfect, I thought. Their raft slid down the left rock and barely missed the churning hole. Three more rafts passed, some hitting and some missing the hole.

Finally, it was our turn. Excitement bubbled up inside me. My teammates and I jogged down the path to our raft and got in. With a history of ear problems, I knew I should not get my ears wet in river or lake water. We anxiously started down the rapids, then just as I heard the falls, I tried desperately to force wax earplugs into my ears as I heard the splashing noise of the falls get louder. The sound of the falls grew louder as we were swept around a turn amidst angry waters. I paddled with all my might, juggling my paddle and my wax, and forcing the wax in halfway. I sat on the edge of my raft, struggling to hold on. Just then my raft turned dangerously sideways. Backwards would be okay, but not sideways. Sideways anything could happen. As the middle paddler–the first to encounter the swirling hole–I suddenly realized my danger. In a matter of seconds I was jerked backwards and swept into the icy swirling water.

We had been sucked into a "hole" where the force of the water can tip a raft easily. Instinct told me to stay calm as I struggled to keep my head above the churning water.

I whipped ahead of my raft as people reached out for me. My ears throbbed as I fought for my safety rope. Mentally I thanked Tim for the rope and the lesson on safety as I was pulled through the icy water to the safety of the shore.

After a nice hot shower and a good night's rest, we were back on the road again. This time our destination was Griff's Fish Camp by the St. Mary's River–one of the many waterways into Okefenokee Swamp, in Southeast Georgia, the next leg of our trip.

We arrived in darkness late at night, and my partners and I quickly pitched our tent. I took some time out to enjoy my surroundings. The area was full of native Spanish moss drooping mysteriously from huge tree branches. The continuous chirping of crickets and the croaks of frogs echoed inside my head. The roar of a bonfire called me even though I already felt warm in the Georgia air.

Red ants found their way onto my toes taking big juicy bites into my flesh, as I searched frantically for the after-bite from the first aid kit. Adding more wood to the already popping and sizzling fire, I gathered around our campfire as Tim explained night-shine. With my flashlight close to my head and next to my eyes, I made my way with my friends, waking slowly, experiencing new night sounds. I found the sounds different than those of the everlasting mountains as I searched for the red shine of alligator eyes in the St. Mary's River.

With my eyes glued on the shine from my flashlight I slowly walked around the area of St. Mary's River at Griff's Fish Camp. "There they are!" The spiders' eyes shimmered in the darkness as the light reflected from their eyes.

I spotted minnows and frogs with my flashlight resting next to my eyes. Next a yellow pair of eyes sneaked out, catching my attention; a fox lingered near. Many animals were up and about in the darkness of midnight.

Later, the quiet of the new morning made me feel so peaceful inside. As my two tent partners awoke, I quietly slipped into my clothes. We quickly dressed and packed, and were the first to break down our tent and help with breakfast to get an early start in our canoes.

The hollow sound of wind through the mighty bald cypress trees of Okefenokee Swamp fascinated me as I steered in the back of my canoe. My partner, Sarah, and I practiced, somewhat awkwardly, with each other, and learned to canoe successfully through the shallow channel, a finger of the great swamp, out to the vast open space of Okefenokee. Swamp grasses and plants grew along the edges, making the going tough.

We plowed through tea-colored water that gets brown from the many decaying plants. I spotted one alligator after another basking in the sun. The mysteriousness of the swamp intrigued me. I wanted to know more about the swamp–its quiet vastness and its many plants and animals. I felt for the swamp, for I know it has not long to live with all the careless people in the world wanting to destroy its beauty and stillness.

An alligator swam right next to my canoe. If I were to just reach my fingertips down, I could have felt its bumpy back. As we moved along, I paddled as quietly as I could, trying to see as much as I could. Huge bald cypress trees loomed overhead with long wisps of gray green Spanish moss dangling from their branches. Small islands dotted the area thick with dense under-growth like cinnamon ferns and other low plants.

The "never-wets" interested me as Tim explained how the plant acquired its name. This plant had a natural waxy substance coating on its leaves and stems, and as I paddled by, I playfully pushed some leaves under the water to see what would happen. Sure enough, they popped back up, totally dry. Next we had to maneuver our canoe out from between two trees.

My stomach rumbled as I heard joyful shouts from other canoes in our party reaching the island. Billy's Island was a welcoming sight to all of us, and we scrambled onto its marshy soil, hungrily helping to prepare a lunch of bagels and cream cheese.

Eagerly, I ripped off my life vest and grabbed lunch. Yum! I was hungry after half a day of canoeing. I took a hike into the wooded area of Billy's Island to take a bathroom break and to rest. In the shade of the towering cypress trees, I felt safe, like nothing could ever happen to me under their watch. They seemed to always be guarding me as I closed my eyes and felt the swamp's presence and fullness. I felt part of the swamp, always growing and maturing.

Back out on the swamp in our canoes, after collecting our meteorological data, the sun, unrelenting, seemed to want me out of its sight. Its rays beat down on my back, and although it was already October, it felt like the hot months of summer.

Two of my teachers who were also canoe partners, Tim and Chris, led us on a narrow, winding channel to a small area of peat called a battery. The swamp was a continuous cycle, always growing and changing.

Peat forms on the bottom of the swamp from decaying plants which is what it is composed of. A blow-up occurs when decomposing gases float some peat to the surface. Soon, some plants will begin to grow in the rich peat on this 'battery.' It is a 'house' as it starts to stabilize and larger plants begin to take root. Finally, it is an 'island' of dryer land that holds many trees and stable plants. But, as every cycle must start over, fires destroy it and it must begin again.

In this very marshy part of the swamp, Sarah and I half paddled and half pushed with our paddles on the mucky bottom, trying to canoe in mud over to the battery. Tim explained how to walk on a battery; you must run quickly over the quaking earth, or you'll fall through the peat into the alligator infested waters. Grabbing my paddle, I plunged out of my canoe onto the unstable peat. This is where I learned how this swamp got its name. Okefenokee means "land of the quaking earth," and I quickly learned that this earth sure was not stable!

Quickly I leaped; my shaky legs began to disappear. Suddenly, 'kerplop!' With my face streaked with mud, I scrambled up out of the hole where I just now sank, only to find myself sinking deeper. My dripping, itching body heaved itself out only to fall into the murky stuff again about five more times as I made my way through the battery back to the safety of my canoe. I pushed the canoe quickly through the sticky grasses to safety.

As we backed out of the channel into the open swamp, a couple of canoes were assigned to stay back to make sure everyone was accounted for. Peacefully, we paddled for a while spotting 'gator after 'gator until we stopped to listen to the beautiful, unique swamp sounds, so unlike any other sounds on earth. The trees seemed to whisper like children late at night. I thought how lucky and special I was to be experiencing and discovering new secrets of this mysterious swamp every minute.

We were about to shove off again when we noticed the canoes that had stayed behind were missing. Great! Tim and a classmate, Michael, went back to get them while we sat and waited. After half an hour, I began to get restless. Suddenly two deer peeked out of the woods. Quietly, I watched them, recognizing now how important the swamp really is. It is a home to many animals and plants, and I felt grateful to experience it and to be a part of it.

"Roarrrr!" That was Tim zooming through the still waters of the swamp in a motorized boat. The missing canoes were too far behind for too long. They thought we had gone all the way back to the beginning of our journey. Well, I tied my bandana over my blistered hand and started paddling back to camp. What a day this had been! I would never forget it.

At our new campsite just outside of Okefenokee Swamp Park, we pitched our tent for the fifth time. We showered with our swimming suits on, and I helped to cook the chicken for supper. Hungry, Kyrstin and I stole tastes of one of our best dinners yet. That night I slept very well after a day of hard work.

In the car again the next day we looked for the first glimpse of the beautiful ocean. We reached the ferry in plenty of time to repack and condense our belongings. Everything we were not going to take was thrown into one of the U-Hauls as we worked together once again to successfully carry everything aboard the ferry. We were going to a beautiful island.

The wind whipped through my hair as we plowed through blue waters. The marshy grass, Spartina Grass, created a channel of ocean for us to follow out to Sapelo Island. As the salt spray splashed my face, I was reminded of all the special times at the ocean chasing crabs, building sand creations, splashing in the shallow salt, and body surfing. I couldn't wait. The ocean called me once again to its beautiful vastness, to what I love and of which I am a part.

Once again we set up our tents and took a night walk out onto the beach. The campsite was very peaceful and some would say, romantic. As we walked along a foot trail about a mile out to the open beach, I knew I was experiencing still another environment. Frogs and crickets sang as the salt grasses swayed with the breeze.

The beach at Sapelo was beautiful with the sunset reflecting on the wet sand and the ocean; I slipped off my sandals and wiggled my toes in the soft, white sand. Ghost crabs scampered in and out of the ocean, but preferred the dry sand. After dinner we went back to the beach for another night walk. I lay down on the soft sand and calmly listened to the sounds of the rolling waves as the very last touches of pink faded away and the stars began to appear over the ever singing ocean.

The night sky has always fascinated me, but on this trip, I had many more experiences to explore this ancient scene. It amazed me to know that the starlight I saw was generated millions of years ago, but is just now reaching the earth. By watching and observing the night sky that night for ten minutes, I saw a shooting star.

I know there are people in many different places who are looking at the same time at the same stars and constellations in the sky as I. In this way, I am connected with others who share this same wonder with me.

Reluctantly, we went back to our campsite. I awoke at dawn to the beeping of my watch alarm telling me and my tent group, Kyrstin and Rachel, that we had fifteen minutes to get dressed and out to the beach for low tide and sunrise. I quickly slipped into my swimsuit, grabbed my towel, and the three of us ran along the path, not wanting to miss anything. Happily we arrived in time and waded out to our ankles in the warm, foaming water. A few lingering clouds twisted and turned creating wonderful pictures in the sky with the soft, but brilliant colors of sunrise. What a joy it was to be living and experiencing this moment! Within only five minutes the ocean was up to my knees as it began the high tide cycle. What a peaceful morning it was with the shore birds calling and the ocean breeze puffing gently on my face.

After breakfast cleanup, we took all of our instruments and trailed down to the salt marsh. This wide, open plane smelled salty as I made my way through its tall grasses. First, we collected the meteorological data necessary and then I squished my way through the muddy earth to find mussels for our dinner. As Tim showed us where to find the clumps of big mussels, I sank deeper into the mushy ground. Connor held the pot of mussels worth cooking, and we took turns throwing the mussels into the pot, trying to make 'baskets.' Suddenly, the mud seemed to be gulping me. I put pressure on my other leg to pull myself out, but only found myself sinking deeper and deeper into the muck. The mud felt cool against my skin from the hot, glaring sun as Kyrstin tried to pull me out. I actually had to reach down with my hands to grab my sandal and lift my foot out. By now I was almost up to my hips in gunky, slimy mud. Finally, with Kyrstin pulling my upper body, and holding onto a sturdy clump of grass, and with me pulling each foot in turn, I was free once again. The sucking sound of the mud stayed in my ears as we stumbled back to shore.

Now we ventured out to the ever-changing ocean. After rinsing off, we seined a tide pool and the ocean itself for crabs and fish. Many of these crabs and mussels later met their death

43

in our pot for supper. Back at the campsite, I helped gut and clean fish, and scrubbed the mussels. I couldn't wait for dinner because I had helped to find it, gather it, clean it, prepare it, and would eat it, too. Knowing I was eating straight from the earth and the sea, and using these prized resources, I felt grateful.

Ahh! The ocean was what I had been waiting for...pounding waves crashed in my ears as I waded in the warm depths after dinner, patiently waiting for a wave to body surf to ride all the way in to shore.

The continuous thunder of the angry waves echoes in my ears.
I am out where it is deep
where the dark waves just begin their furl.
Calmly, I watch and wait.
I wait for the perfect wave to come, for
one that can bring me in, all the way in, in to shore,
in to the sand
and foam of the clear blue water. Finally, I am rewarded.
The perfect wave is approaching.
Naturally, I dive, stretching out in
a swift line as the wave curls around me,
inviting me to know
the feeling of being part of the ocean,
to know and understand
the delicate ecosystem–
one so delicate that if the wave is not
just right, or my dive not perfect, I will not succeed.
To know. To feel. To live.

Swiftly, I ride over the water
with endless speed steering around
a group of people I had seen beforehand
by leaning my weight,
and surely curving my path. I seem to become
part of the twisting
waters, part of the wave itself. This is as close as

I have come to flying free. Free.
The word again becomes real. I coast on the
crest of the wave, leaving all worries
behind in the curling foam
as I race over the endless waters.
Not knowing if I am two inches
or two feet away from the sandy bottom, I am flung into the
frothy foam as my lungs gasp for air, air that once was mine
but was taken in exchange for the ride. Proudly, I stand up,
dripping with salt water, with sand burns
on my shins, knowing
that I knew. I have flown. I have been part
of the world itself.
Free.

After a cozy fireside game, we were up once more and on our way out to the bridge. This was a tradition of The College School–to share our reflections of our Field Ecology experiences with one another at the bridge. We threw stones over the railing into the water below watching tiny, microscopic animals glow, giving off light when bumping into things or each other.

Gathering in a circle on the bridge, we each told how we had overcome challenges, and from those experiences had grown closer together as a class, and had learned more about each other and ourselves. It was a special time.

Up the next day at 6:00 a.m. to witness the beauty of the morning sky, I knew it was to be our last day on the island. The clouds glowed with light. One look away meant missing wonderful images. Beneath the brilliant rays of the morning sun we wrote with our toes and fingers in the wet sand, memorizing Sapelo's beauty. Never will I forget its long, empty beaches crying for attention, its barren salt marshes and its lonely sand dunes, or its ocean.

We swam under the hot sun in crashing waves again today. The ocean seemed to go on forever as we wished the day would. I came up only for quick gulps of air as I crashed into

45

shore, whizzing past others. I loved body surfing. I loved riding the waves into shore. My friends challenged me, but I won easily, beached on the scratchy sand ahead of them each time.

Reluctantly, we took one last look at Sapelo as we packed and piled into the bus. We took the ferry to the mainland. Back in the van we drove many hours, stayed the night in a motel, and explored the Tennessee Aquarium to wrap up our trip with all of its experiences still fresh in our minds. Then we traveled another whole day back to St. Louis. Home. I haven't thought of that word, home, in over a week. But I'll soon be there.

From being on top of the world, to keeping my head above the swirling threatening water, to floating in a delicate ecosystem, to mud gulping me and to swimming with the powerful waves, I have learned how to accept challenges and make the most of my experiences. I meet the world at its most beautiful, and become part of it.

I become part of the mountain, feeling the hot and dry sun on my back all day long. Like the rocks, I am stubborn, not willing to lose my courage, promising myself I will make it to the top.

I become part of the river as I dance and splash, overcoming the obstacles of rocks. I dash down life's path as I hurry on to the next challenge.

I become part of the swamp, always changing, growing, and maturing. I am full of life as I learn to cope with many hardships, but find there are many different ways to live and adapt to my surroundings.

I become part of the salt marsh, slowing down at times, but teeming with life at others. I shift and struggle as I learn to live between two different environments.

I become part of the ocean. I plunge into the watery depths and roll and crash in fury.

I come and go as the days pass, giving birth to many new ideas. This is what life is all about.

As I meet the world at its most I find who I really am and where I fit in as I strive to overcome many challenges and to succeed.

Michelle Marincel

Michelle Marincel was born on September 12, 1983, and lives in St. Louis, Missouri. She attends a private school, The College School of Webster Groves, Missouri, where she is in the eighth grade. She is strong in language arts and is always writing new poems, stories, and songs. She is a part of the Middle School Literary Magazine; she is also in ST-ART, a gifted art program with her local public school district. She has been playing the violin for ten years, and is in the first violin section in an orchestra with the St. Louis Symphony Music School. She also enjoys playing piano.

Michelle is part of the Middle School ensemble and plays Orf instruments, marimbas, and a variety of band and percussion instruments. Michelle acts in many all-school assemblies and is always willing to help within her school community. She plays softball, basketball, and tennis. She also swims and ice skates.

An Appalachian Experience

*Jamiyla amazes herself on her adventure
with Outward Bound.*

by Jamiyla Bolton

One day in May of 1997, I was lying on the couch sick when my mother came home from work and told me that I had been awarded a scholarship for a program called Outward Bound. At the time, my 101 degree fever did not allow me to process my thoughts very well, but later on, when I felt better, I remembered the application and essay I had sent to the Raleigh Police Department. I would get a chance to, as I said in my essay, "experience new things."

I would be spending sixteen days in Asheville, North Carolina, mountain climbing, hiking, and surviving in the wilderness. I was told the trip would be difficult, but looking back, I think extreme would be a better word.

The trip was to begin on August 7th. I was not happy about cutting off my yearly visit to New York by two weeks but my mother convinced me that I had been chosen and that it was an honor to have gotten the scholarship, so I decided to go. After all, I could always go to New York, but the trip with Outward Bound would be a once in a lifetime experience.

I got a long list of supplies for the trip, and some tips on how to prepare. While I was in New York, I ran twelve laps around the track three or four times a week. That summer passed by quickly and before I knew it, it was August 6th.

With a few tears in my eyes, I got on an Amtrak train in New York and went back to Raleigh. I ate my final meal of home cooked food and took my last real shower–it would be sixteen days before I would do that again–and tried to prepare myself for the plane ride. Flying was going to be an adventure in itself because I was more of a ground person. On the plane, I gripped the seat in front of me and didn't let go until we landed. When I finally got to Asheville an hour later (it seemed like forever), I nearly kissed the ground!

After a long bus ride from the airport, I arrived at the base camp. All the teenagers there split up into "crews" of eleven, and I met the instructors. My instructors were Greg, Buck, and Olia. Next we all got to know all of the crew members. There were eleven of us in all, with four girls and seven guys. After receiving our gear and our huge backpacks, we set up camp, ate noodles with parmesan cheese and went to bed.

Next morning we woke up early to do a team incentive that was to help get us to work together as a team. All of us–Fabiola, Linsey, Charlotte, Josh, Alex with the hat, Alex, Robert, John, and Francisco–had to get over this log that was high up in some trees. We had to learn to get along because we would be each other's only family for two weeks.

After we had all gotten over the log, we packed food and went to a campsite off-base. We would start our expedition the next day.

We woke up at six to begin our hike. We walked for what seemed about ten hours and got only five miles up the trail because we kept stopping to rest. We tried to encourage each other, but only Linsey had enough pep to keep saying, "C'mon guys, you can do it," even when she wanted to stop.

Carolina to Georgia without a trail! With people falling out from exhaustion, the crew had a heavier load to carry. We all wanted to cry. It was one o'clock in the morning when we finally got to our camp site and slept. When we got up the next morning, all we did was hike about a mile to an open watchtower called Raban Bald. I could see the clear sky and the stars, and for the first time I was actually glad I did not stay in New York. This was different and special.

We were given our destination for our final expedition the next day. It was supposed to take us two days, but we decided to complete it in one so we could rest. That day was hard!

We were forced (by our instructors) to hike down a ridge so steep we could barely walk without falling. Linsey's ankles gave out; Charlotte got stung by bees; and I was constantly getting hit in the face by tree branches. We did have fun later running through this open field while the moon was bright. We got to sleep late that night, but the next day had a day full of sleeping late, resting, eating, and swimming. From then on, I thought everything would be a piece of cake. I was wrong.

On the eighth day of the trip, we built an extension of the Appalachian trail. This meant moving rocks out of the way and clearing the trail to make a nice path for hikers. That afternoon we all thought we would be returning to the base camp, but instead we went back to the place where we had started our expedition. There we were each given a little bag with an apple, some peanuts, a bagel, and a small chunk of cheese, and told we were to go on a *solo*. For the solo each one of us was alone in the woods for two whole days and one night, and with bees and snakes everywhere, I was really scared. I was bored too because the time passed slowly. I tried to sleep a lot and I wrote in my journal until the days passed. When the solo was finally over, we all ate together and went back to base camp for the last week of the trip.

We woke up early that morning to start mountain climbing. After learning the basics, we went to a certain rock to practice climbing. I was very good at it. I found a talent I never knew I had and it was fun. The following day we climbed on a bigger rock, and on the final day of climbing we went to White Rock, a real mountain. It was very steep and difficult to climb, and I came close to falling many times. Once we got to the top we could rappel down. I rappelled down; rappelling is a fun way to get down quickly by a rope. Of all the things I did at Outward Bound, rock climbing with rappelling is the thing I might take up as a hobby some day. Looking up at the mountain after rappelling, I was sad because now my favorite part of the trip was over.

With only three days left in the trip I began to like being on the trip with Outward Bound. We did a ropes course high up in the air, and I was very afraid at first. Once I got into it, I had fun. I even swung down from 200 feet up on a rope like Tarzan. The day after that we ran a seven and a half mile mini-marathon in which I came in second out of all the girls. Then we cleaned and returned all our gear and had a big farewell party. We all cried.

I appreciated the trip a lot more once I had left. I would do it again, too, but I just need twenty years or so to recover. I learned so much about myself on that trip. I learned I could, and still can, do anything I put my mind to. I also realized the importance of teamwork. I could not have survived without the help and encouragement of my crew. I found a new talent, and made friends. I still write and call Linsey.

But I also learned that everyone will not always be on my side. In the diverse group, some people did not like females who took charge and some did not like African Americans, which is what I am. But that is how the world is.

I had no female role models but myself. I learned to believe in me, and in what I could do. Females have to realize that no one can hold them back from doing anything they put their minds to. Anything can be an adventure, and although something like an airplane ride might be small to one person, it might be a major accomplishment for another. Just take any challenge–and never cease to amaze yourself.

Jamiyla Bolton

Jamiyla Haliyma Bolton was born on December 7, 1982, in Brooklyn, New York. Now sixteen, she resides in a housing community called Walnut Terrace in Raleigh, North Carolina, with her mother, her sisters Raquiyba, Aisha, and Atiya, and her brother Hasan. The other members of her family currently reside in New York. She attends William G. Enloe High School, where she is a member of the track team, the African American Female Enrichment Organization, and Spanish Club.

Jamiyla is athletic, courageous, and fun. She likes to take challenges and do things she's never done before. Taken from one of her adventures, her motto is to never cease to amaze herself.

Cross-Country Cycling

Sarabeth builds her physical and mental strength by getting to camp the hard way.

by Sarabeth Matilsky

I was in the Seattle Airport anticipating my red-eye flight home to the East Coast with very little joy. I was returning to New Jersey from a camp for homeschooled teenagers, and it had been an incredible week. What a bummer to end all that with a trip on something as sterile as an *airplane.*

And then suddenly, all the inspiration that had surrounded me for the last week bubbled up in the form of a dream which soon became a plan: I would ride my bike to camp next year! I rather surprised myself for a minute, but that was that. No matter that I'd barely ridden more than fifteen miles at one time on a bicycle; no matter that I knew next to nothing about bike mechanics and even less about bicycle touring; I just knew in a flash that I was going to ride my bike across the country from the East Coast to the West Coast next summer.

In the twelve months that followed, preparations took a great deal of my energy. I spent my time working to make money, pouring over huge books about touring and mechanics, apprenticing at my local bike store to expand my *(very)* rudimentary knowledge of bicycles, buying gear, and contacting homeschool families with whom I wished to stay along the way. I began to feel pangs of self-doubt as the enormity of my plans began to hit me.

During this time some people made negative comments about my trip, feeling it was their duty to warn me of all the dangers out there; however, many other people gave me whole-hearted support. My family, though they had their own worries, blessed me with their trust. And once on the road, my twice-weekly phone calls home were one comforting constant in my world of variables. I also gained inspiration in the months before I left from several people, one of whom was a woman named Kyla Wetherell. Kyla, at age sixteen, had ridden a bicycle around South America alone for a year. I thought of the strength she needed to go on her journey, and that helped me when the going got tough for my own trip. At the beginning of March I wrote in my journal:

> *In the last few weeks, especially, I've felt like there is a rope tied around me, pulling me inexorably toward the crevasse that lies between myself now and something else. Adulthood? Lately that rope has been tugging so hard at times, making me scramble over and around all sorts of physical and mental obstacles. I just have to go.*

So I went. On Saturday, March 24, 1997, I boarded a bus with my bicycle and we headed towards Yorktown, Virginia, to begin our cross-country journey. I planned on using the Trans America bike route, a network of public roads that was put together in 1976 by the ACA and has since been used by thousands of cyclists over the last twenty years. It is over 4,200 miles long and passes through ten states: Virginia, Kentucky, Illinois, Missouri, Kansas, Colorado, Wyoming, Montana, Idaho, and Oregon. From my journal, Sunday, March 31st, I wrote:

My campsite last night was a sand pit with no drainage. It rained buckets and buckets, and though my tent didn't leak, I didn't sleep much. I could feel water sloshing under my nylon floor and I worried that the tarp might have blown off my bike which was leaning against a nearby picnic table. As soon as the sun rose, I left, pedaling my trusty gray Panasonic out into the hazy Virginia morning. But as the sun continued to rise, the wind began to blow hard and right in my face. In fact, every time I changed direction it seemed as though the wind always turned too, trying to push me backwards, back to the coast, back home to N.J., back to the time before I'd ever decided to go on this stupid bike trip in the first place. But I kept cranking, up the hills, down the hills, through the deserted and brown not-yet-springtime of the rural south. Then, in Scotchtown, I stopped in a little grocery store–which was the whole town, as far as I could tell–to use the facilities.

The woman behind the counter directed me through the stockroom at the back of the store, and when I found the bathroom, I looked down and saw that I'd gotten my period. I groaned, went out to my right rear bike bag to get my tampons, and it was back onto my saddle again–for four more hours. Dogs chased me and thunder boomed menacingly not too far away. I pedaled for what seemed like eternity. But I had to get to my campsite, that much was clear in my mind, and I pushed the pedals around and around and around and around....

March 31st was the eighth day of my cross-country bike trip, and it was the first day of many when I wondered to myself, "Why on earth did I want to do this?" Sweaty and exhausted, both physically and mentally, I arrived at my destination that chilly, windy March afternoon after having to walk the last two miles because of a gravel road. And then I began to understand why people down through the ages have pushed themselves to physical and emotional extremes while in search of challenge and adventure. As I stood there with my bicycle, at the end of my day's ride, a warm glow began to come from my heart and spread throughout my body. I could feel it from the top of my head to the tips of my toes, a feeling of intense satisfaction and incredulity that I had *made* it.

Of course, every new day of my trip brought its own challenges–and I came to see that it would never be *easy*–that riding was instead gradations of challenge. But each night brought an ever-growing craving for more of the physical difficulty that inevitably brought that warm glow, and the knowledge that I was strong and my body was beautiful, not because of how it looked but because of what it could do for me.

Although I was technically riding alone, I always found that just as I reached a point in my trip where I thought I simply could not go on, I met someone–or several people–who helped me to get over the hump. In Carbondale, Illinois, I met Jeff Amaral and Wyeth Friday, riding towards Oregon. We talked for two hours on a rainy May evening, and decided to ride together the next day. Wyeth and Jeff were patient with my slower pace and I was very happy to be traveling with them. We rode together until the end of June. The steep climbs in the Ozarks and the heat of Kansas and eastern Colorado were made more enjoyable with Jeff's jokes and Wyeth's steady pedaling in the front of our little group.

Two things set me apart from many of the other cyclists that I met in my five month journey. First, I was young (seventeen) and second, I was female and traveling by myself. I realized shortly after my trip began that very few women go cycle touring alone. I didn't meet a single female cyclist until Kansas, and I met only two women on the entire trip who were riding alone. I interacted primarily with men–men in stores, men at gas stations, or other male cyclists, and although I was usually treated with respect, there were times when I wasn't. I felt fear sometimes too, and I mostly felt alone in my fear.

Calling home was great, but sometimes I craved contact with other women whose first question was something other than, "Aren't you scared?" I wanted someone to say, "I'm doing that too...and you're right...it *is* hard sometimes to be alone and get one's period while riding or get whistled at by obnoxious men or feel the need to prove oneself in order to be treated with respect.... But you know what? You can do it!"

I met Wally in Montana, just as I was leaving the campground in the morning. A blue bike was leaning up against the restroom with a sticker on the top-tube that read "Wild Woman." As I talked with Wally I saw a petite, blond, woman in her thirties who did not appear at first glance to be especially wild. But then Wally told me where she was going. In three summers–this being her second–she planned to ride alone from the top of Alaska in North America all the way down to the bottom of Chile in South America! Although our conversation lasted only an hour, her exuberance and courage were reassuring; they helped center me and gave me renewed confidence in myself. When we rode off in opposite directions, Wally gave me an owl feather she had found by which to remember her.

After I met Wally, I continued my journey to Oregon. I pedaled up many more mountains in those last few weeks, met many more wonderful, caring people, and on August fifteenth, I reached the sand dunes of the coast of Oregon. When I scrambled up the dunes and caught sight of the ocean I was laughing and crying at the same time. I started to run down, and ran and ran and ran to meet the sea, not really believing I was there until I felt its shocking cold and wetness on my body. My last journal entry was just these three words: *I did it*.

   Now that I'm home for awhile, I keep that owl feather up in my room to remind me of the perseverance, exuberance, courage, and strength I found within myself that summer. It reminds me of everything that is possible, both for me in my life and for all women, as we ride our "bicycles" over all sorts of mountains. I know at times we'll get saddle sores along the way, but I believe that we'll keep riding anyway. We can't help it. We have the constant allure of the open road ahead of us, and no one–not *anything*–can stop us.

Sarabeth Matilsky

When not off on an adventure, Sarabeth Matilsky lives in Highland Park, New Jersey, with her parents, three younger brothers, one younger sister, and five cats. Sarabeth was born November 12, 1979. She and her younger siblings have been homeschooled all their lives, which has meant learning not only at home, but also in libraries, theaters, museums, the local food co-op, and the nearby university. As a family, they take cross-county camping trips, go ice-skating with friends, and go to dance, art, and music classes, as well as sports practices.

The freedom, trust, and responsibility Sarabeth's parents have given her have allowed her to take charge of her education and pursue many interests, which include ballet, modern and improvisational dance, reading books of every description, singing folk songs and rounds with friends, writing essays when inspiration hits, creating wire sculptures and mobiles, making mixed-media collages, and traveling–especially by bicycle!

Backpacking in the West

Lindsay takes a break before college to put her mind and body to the test.

by Lindsay Citerman

I made the decision to do something cool and outdoors for the summer after my senior year when I realized that I would be heading off to school far away in a few months after having led a fairly static life. I had been in the same school system since kindergarten and had spent the last eight summers with the same friends at the same camp in the Northwoods of Minnesota. Camp had been somewhat of a challenge when I was ten years old but over the years it had become less of an experience in nature and more of a month without parents and with best friends I did not get to see during the regular school year. I wanted to try something new before going off to college. I think I also wanted to practice being with new people. I had never had trouble acquiring new friends but I could not remember the last time I had been in a situation where I didn't know anyone.

Mostly, though, I wanted to go out into the woods on some intense program that would test my body and mind to the limits. I have always been fairly athletic and into working my body, but I had never really had the means or experience to do any of the extreme sports. I researched a bunch of programs and finally decided on a National Outdoor Leadership School (NOLS) program in the Rocky Mountains. The program consisted of 29 days in the middle of the summer backpacking through the Beartooth and Absoroka ranges in Wyoming and Montana.

I really tried to prepare for the trip but I did not do all that much. I was used to running every day so I thought that was quite enough. Mentally I was not preparing for the trip at all. The first month and a half of summer were some of the best times I had ever had with my friends. I went out constantly and gave no thought whatsoever to the impending 30 days when I would be totally out of contact.

The morning I was leaving, I could not have been more ready to get out in the mountains; I was absolutely psyched, although I had no idea what to expect. When I arrived and met my group I was even more excited. Ironically, my group consisted of eleven women and only three men, including the leaders. The leaders, one male and one female, told us that most trips were primarily male. There were all women trips specifically designated by NOLS that attract more women. To be honest, all women trips did not interest me at all.

I really went into this trip knowing that I am as tough as any male when it comes to basic survival. Why should it matter if there were men on the trip? But as we got ready to go we had meetings and such about possible group dynamics between the sexes. This was not even an issue for me. I definitely think my whole group felt the same way. Maybe it was because there were so many women who were already pretty tough, but there was really no sexual bias from any member of the group. I also think that NOLS planned well by having one female leader and one male leader, particularly the two who were assigned to our trip. Both leaders were physically ready to take on anything and neither one possessed extreme sex differentiating characteristics–no Superman and no delicate female stuff either.

Basic daily activities once we were in the field consisted of hiking, camping, and studying the environment around us. The main goal of the trip was to teach us how to survive in the woods. In the beginning, we learned simple things like how to load our packs and how to go to the bathroom in the woods in a way that is safest for the environment. From there, we moved on to map reading and, eventually, we traveled in small groups for a couple of days without our leaders.

Every day was a different challenge. There were days when I thought my legs were going to fall off. About nine days into the trip I got three blisters which stayed with me for the rest of the month. I think some of my most trying moments on the trip were made ten times more of a challenge because of the constant pain in my feet–and when I say pain I mean indescribable agony pulsing throughout both feet. I just had to tell myself to keep going.

The most incredible part of the trip was learning about the power of my mind. For example, one day we hiked 2,500 feet up in elevation that represented over one and a half miles of bushwhacking. The steepness of the mountain at this point was from 6O-8OE. The terrain was unsteady and difficult with either lots of deadfall or no trees at all and loose rock. Also, on this particular day water was at a minimum; we each had one bottle of water to last for the entire hike. I was dehydrated and tired with a fifty pound pack to carry. One hiker is supposed to be able to carry 30% of his own body weight, but because of the group size, I was carrying about 50% of my body weight. I remember exactly what if felt like for my throat to be that dry and for my legs and back to be constantly in pain.

At the same time it was incredible. I just kept telling myself to keep moving and climbing. It was slow and steady. I did not say a word for the entire second half of the climb and I hurt a lot, but the feeling I had when I finished was amazing.

That was how I would characterize the entire trip. I can't describe my feelings in words, but I know I have been a different person ever since that month. I came to college with a renewed sense of who I was and what I wanted to do. It was a month of physical challenge, but it was also a month of finding personal clarity. I set out to do something that was a true test of my entire being both mentally and physically. And as soon as I had showered for the first time in thirty days, I was ready to go back out and do it all over again.

Lindsay Citerman

Lindsay Citerman was born on March 12, 1978. She grew up in Clayton, Missouri, where she lived with her parents and an older brother. She attended the same school from kindergarten through high school with people she had known her whole life. She attended summer camp in Minnesota every summer.

Lindsay enjoys running, reading, and relaxing outside. She played varsity field hockey in high school and participated in a variety of clubs including the environmental organization at her high school. She was heavily involved in planning an arts fair for special students at her school each spring.

Lindsay is a boisterous, outgoing person. She likes to challenge herself physically and push her body to the limit. She loves being outside and is completely comfortable living in the woods. At present, Lindsay attends Columbia University in New York City. At Columbia, she has been involved with the hiking and biking programs and has participated in the outdoor orientation programs which take incoming freshmen on outdoor orientation trips.

Caving

Dana overcomes her insecurities and leads others in an adventure.

by Dana Romanoff

I can see nothing. I mean, absolutely nothing. It is so dark that I cannot see my hand just inches from my face. I feel only the granite–slick and rimy with ice–pressing hard on my shoulders and back. No air moves–just cold all around. I strain to hear a noise, but hear only my breathing. A child whispers, "Mommy, I'm scared." The mother breathes a nervous laugh. There is silence and darkness. I am also scared. Finally, after an endless time, a beam of light slices the darkness. It is my partner, Sean. He has found the tunnel exit among the side passages and dead ends.

It was time to move on. There was still much more to explore in Double Birches, the ice cave atop Chirnney Mountain in the Adirondacks of upper New York State. This was my first time leading the caving trip and I was just as frightened as the others. There was no one for me to hold onto, or to guide me. This was my new job. Sean led the way and I brought up the rear, coaxing the guests from Timberlock Lodge to move carefully and keep their heads down. On our hands and knees, we scrambled over rock outcroppings we could not see. The flashlights did little but illuminate our breath hanging thick like steam in the air. Bodies molded to fit an impossibly narrow passage, and then expanded on the other side. We were about to enter the cavern. I moved to the front of the group and pulled myself over a crack in the floor of the cave offering my hand to bring the adventurers up over the brink. Someone dislodged some pebbles; an avalanche of them rained down the chasm. We never heard them hit bottom. I did not tell the cavers that the bottom is sixty feet below.

We entered the main room of the cave, and my body was thankful for the space. My skin loosened and I was able to breathe deeply. The beam of my flashlight skipped from rock to rock as the granite walls reluctantly gave up their secrets. To the left, an icicle briefly appeared. To the right, a huge stalagmite was waiting as if to impale an innocent victim. The light was extinguished, amplifying the sounds of darkness. There was a hush as the rhythmic dripping of melting ice echoed against the walls.

People were anxious and chilled—not from the cold, but from being too long in a foreign and desolate world. We shone our flashlights toward the exit. It was a tight, steep climb out of Double Birches and there was only one way to negotiate the icy pitch. In a reassuring, confident voice that I did not recognize as my own, I instructed, "Find a crack over to the left where you can wedge your fingers; then pull up and find the foothold by your right hip; trust the rock and reach for my wrist." Around the bend was the first crack of daylight.

The air was much warmer above. We stripped off our layers and enjoyed the security of the forest with its familiar sights and sounds. Children stood bug-eyed as their parents' knees still wobbled. They had a chance to explore a part of the world few get to know.

As I stood outside the cave I exalted in my good fortune. Instead of spending my summers flipping burgers under the golden arches, I spent my summers doing things I love, under golden skies in the Adirondack Mountains.

Leading the group down the steep trail, I felt proud. I had discovered strengths I never knew I had. At first I was frightened of the responsibility of leading an expedition, knowing that parents were depending on me to guide and teach them and their children. I had to overcome my insecurity, and in doing so I found I was a strong and capable leader. I know that the confidence and assurance I displayed in the cave would become a part of my personality.

I learned that exploring caves is related to exploring myself. The terrain often brings surprises, knowledge, and insight.

Dana Romanoff

Dana Romanoff was born in Delmar, New York, in 1978. Her parents' love of the outdoors inspired Dana's enthusiasm for outdoor adventures. Dana has always been involved in activities and sports such as horseback riding, soccer, lacrosse, skiing, mountaineering, rock climbing, etc. She worked at a rustic resort in the Adirondack Mountains of New York State leading hikes, horseback trail rides, waterskiing, caving, and other expeditions, and has worked as a ski instructor.

Just recently, Dana attended the National Outdoor Leadership School Outdoor Educator Course and traversed the Olympic Mountains of Washington State–reaching the summit of Mt. Olympus. Currently, Dana is a student at the University of Rochester in New York where she has devised her own interdisciplinary major on the Study and the Representation of Contemporary Issues in American Culture. She is interning at Blue Jean Magazine, an advertisement-free magazine for teen girls. For her next adventure, she is planning to study abroad. Dana would like to continue in outdoor education and her adventures out west. Dana's passion is photography, especially photographing her own adventures!

Section I
(continued)

Girls' Stories:
International Adventures

A Peruvian Adventure

Exploring marine life in a faraway land led Adriane to appreciate life and nature.

by Adriane C. Lavieri

I wanted my summer to be special, so we decided to visit my mother's home country, Peru. Peru is a beautiful place located on the western side of South America. I traveled 4,000 miles from Maine to Peru. After I arrived, I began visiting family, friends, and historic and local places in the capital, Lima. After a while, I asked my mom about exploring nature in Peru. We looked for many places, but I finally suggested going to the ocean. I wanted to see the wildlife there. We were told that three hours from Lima by bus was a coastal town of Paracas, home to a Pre-Columbian civilization also called Paracas. Not only that, but there also were groups of islands an hour from the coast where wildlife was untouched by civilization. With creatures of the sea living in their natural habitat, it is considered a "World Natural Park" since it belongs to humanity, not just to Peruvians.

I was very excited–so excited that I could hardly sleep during the days before our trip; I dreamed about dolphins, whales, walruses, seals, and the whole marine world. We got prepared by reading about it, checking maps, and asking for information.

71

The hardest thing would be riding in a small boat, rocked by the waves, and hoping the sea would be calm.

I got the courage to go because I had already traveled 4,000 miles. Not to experience what I like most–wildlife and nature–would have been silly. I knew it was not going to be easy; Peru is not the United States, but I thought I could do it. I had been living inland since I was born, and I wanted so much to enjoy life in the sea; it is a world that I haven't been much exposed to–something new and real.

To go on the boat without accidents, we had to skip breakfast. We left the hotel at 7:00 a.m., and traveled to the beach for 45 minutes. There we waited for the boat that left shore at 8:00 a.m. We arrived at the islands at 9:00 a.m. and stayed until 11:00 a.m., enjoying the view, the rock formations, the marine life, and the birds which from the distance seemed like walls on top of the islands. Time flew!

What we saw was nature in its purest form. I was too young to scuba dive, but next time I will do it. I wanted so badly to pat the baby seals on the head, and I tried to reach as far as I could, but it was not possible. I was so happy to see that they were happy too. They were playing around our boat, not afraid of us. They trusted and liked us.

We also saw one of the ancient mysteries of Pre-Columbian civilizations in Peru. We saw "The Chandelier," a figure made thousands of years ago, which still lies on the side of a sandy hill next to the ocean. It is perfect, as if you would have drawn it on paper. It is a mystery, and nobody can explain with certainty its origin and how it has lasted that long.

What I learned is that nature can take care of itself. We saw thousands of families of birds, sea lions, walruses, seals, crabs, mussels, and all kinds of miniature creatures of the sea. We saw what our guide called "the nursery." It was a rock on which only baby seals were allowed. You could see the seal pups play-ing, taking in sun, sleeping, and nursing from the female seals.

I learned that I am able to live under different circumstances now. I am not afraid of the unknown; I enjoy it. I had to stand long walks under the sun, up and down the rocky mountains on the coast, to reach places like the seal nursery where there is nothing but marine life. The air was so special–pure and salty.

Anything could have happened on the trip, from bad weather to motion sickness, or just being scared of being on the ocean for three hours with nothing around but the guides and tourists. But I had my mind set to do it, and my mother was with me. That was enough. My mom helped me all the way; she encouraged me, and told me that this was an opportunity of a lifetime, and that she didn't believe many kids my age would be that adventurous.

Yes, I would do it again many times over, because it takes a brave person to do what I did. I enjoyed it very much and learned to appreciate life and nature. I think that when I grow up, I would like to work in a place where I can take care of the animals of the sea.

My female role models are my mom and my grandmother. They are as adventurous as I am. My mother is a Peruvian lawyer who married an Italian-American and came to the U.S. She has had many accomplishments in a country different from her own.

I would advise others that if you have the opportunity to go to another place, enjoy the adventures that the place offers. If you live in a small place like I do, there are not many opportunities to be adventurous, but you can create your own. Humans have been given a wonderful and mysterious world to live in, and sometimes we take it for granted. Nature is a gift of God, and we should appreciate and take care of it.

Adriane C. Lavieri

Adriane C. Lavieri was born on September 6, 1990, in the city of Torrington, Connecticut. Her parents are William, who is of Italian descent, and Carmen, who is of Spanish descent. She feels very blessed for having such a rich heritage. Her father is self-employed and her mother is a lawyer who teaches at college.

Adriane loves science and the arts. She likes to explore new things, to discover something new everyday, and to learn. At school, she enjoys math, reading, spelling, arts, and music. She lives in a small rural town that is nice and safe. She also is very stubborn because when she puts her mind into something she wants, she usually gets it. She is sensitive and doesn't like to be hurt or to hurt people.

Adriane thinks she is a good adventurer because she is very inquisitive and does not take no for an answer when she wants to find something out.

Solo by Freighter
to South America

*Nellie boards a freighter and heads
to new lands with the crew.*

by Nellie Kelly

Jimmy Buffet's songs about boats, pirates, and hopping on freighters inspired me to take the adventure of a lifetime. Unlike most of the characters in Buffet's songs, I wasn't totally fed up with my day-to-day routine, but I had a deep sense of an impending rut that would only deepen as time went on.

I was 19 and about to finish my second year of community college in Itawamba County, Mississippi. Soon I would transfer to a larger school, start working, and start a family. That plan–that dream–was great in every way except one. It would not allow time for a long vacation. I decided that if I wanted to disappear for a while and see the world, the time would be the summer of 1995, and not a moment later!

I checked out the only book I could find on freighter travel, which was printed in the 1970's when freighter travel peaked. From that book, I found the address of Freighter World Cruises in Pasadena, California. This company, which schedules voyages ranging from three weeks to several months on ships that carry goods from the United States to ports around the world, sent me a fax outlining various departures and destinations.

I knew I had to get serious about saving $2,000 and about getting the nerve to leave all alone with a crew I didn't know on a ship I knew nothing about to countries I didn't know and where I didn't speak the language.

I decided I'd take the trip from Florida to New York and then down the eastern coast of South America. That voyage was the most practical for me because the two-month duration was right and because it departed from Florida, which was a closer flight than to the West Coast.

My vacation was wonderful. Even though I was lonely and scared the first few days, I quickly felt at home and adventurous. I soon learned the names of the five German and Polish officers and fifteen Filipino crewmen. I learned how to play their thirteen-card poker game and video games so I could stay up with them late at night. I also started hanging out with the cook and steward in the kitchen. They taught me new recipes and let me bake bread and cakes, which made me very popular on the ship.

One lesson I learned quickly on the ship was that exciting moments were few and far between, so I took advantage of every opportunity to work in the kitchen and to socialize. But mostly I filled my days reading, cross stitching, getting a tan, washing my clothes in the ship's laundromat, and watching for whales and porpoises. Usually I stayed in my comfortable cabin which was complete with bedroom, closet, shower, table, couch, refrigerator, CD player, radio, and two large windows. Other times I stayed outside on the deck or in the big recreation room where the crew gathered at night.

Every part of life aboard the ship *Altonia* was exceptional, especially the food. Archie, the chef, prepared three great meals a day and dished out ice cream on Sunday afternoons. I lived for Sundays. I ate in the dining room with the officers. Our meals consisted of salad, meat, a vegetable, bread, fruit, and soup. Because my ship life was fairly sedentary, each evening I walked around the 400-foot ship ten times for exercise. But the food was so good, I still gained eight pounds!

My wonderful experiences were equally divided between learning about the ship and seeing the sights when we reached each port. Usually we stayed in each port city an entire day and left the next morning, but in some ports, we stayed only six hours. Walking through the cities fascinated me. Although I couldn't talk to the people I saw, I enjoyed seeing how they lived. I did not see huge hotels and shopping malls because the port cities weren't tourist destinations. I felt almost like an explorer watching real people living their real lives.

I miss the countries I visited and all the guys on the *Altonia*. They were so much fun and so kind to me. They all taught me a great deal about getting along with others, making friends from other cultures, watching star formations, steering a ship, and playing poker. What made my voyage with them even more enjoyable was that I think they liked me, too. We all entertained each other. They fascinated me, and I was a new addition to the ship family whom they enjoyed taking along for the ride.

If you'd like to take a similar freighter trip, I have a few suggestions:

1. Don't worry yourself sick. Any adventure includes risks. When you board a freighter, you don't know what to expect; however I quickly learned that my concerns of being killed and thrown overboard were totally unfounded. The sailors are gentlemen who are happy to teach you about the ship and the cities you visit. And the captain usually puts up with no loose conduct. If any of the crew gives you trouble, tell the captain, and he'll take care of the situation immediately.

2. Learn as much about the ship as possible. Ask the engineer for a tour of the engine room. Use the bridge as a classroom. Ask the captain and first mate to show you how to plot the course, watch for other ships, and use all the gadgets. If you can't sleep at night, go to the bridge; someone will always be there. Help the cook in the kitchen. Stay active so you won't get bored during the one or two week journey between the United States and the first foreign port. If you usually have trouble staying active at home, or if you can't enjoy a little peace and quiet, a freighter might not be for you. Remember, unlike a cruise liner, no one has the job of entertaining you. The crew's job is to see that cargo gets to port. They want you to be happy, but they don't have the resources to play shuffleboard and prepare beverages all day, although they are happy to include you in their karaoke, video games, and poker.

3. Wake up early at least one day a week so the steward can clean your room and put clean sheets on the bed. He comes every day, but if your door is closed, he'll leave.

4. Take your favorite music tapes and a tape player. CDs skip too much on a rough sea to be practical. Music on tape will relax you and remind you of home when you get lonely. Might I suggest Jimmy Buffet? Take some books to read to keep your mind occupied, too.

5. Make friends. The crew will be your brothers, friends, even doctors during the trip, so make an effort to know them well.

6. In port, get off the ship and walk around. I never called for a taxi to take me from the ship to the downtown area. I just started walking. Use your best judgment about safety.

7. Take comfortable shoes and clothes appropriate for the climate where you'll go. I went to South America in May, June, and July. Usually I wore shorts and shirts, but the night air on the ship sometimes was very cold, so take a jacket and jeans, too.

8. You'll be surprised how many international crewmen speak at least a little English, so talk to them. When you walk along the ports, you'll meet men from other ships from all around the world. Take a minute to say, "Hi."

9. Remember, this is your adventure, so enjoy every minute of it–even the times when you have absolutely nothing to do. How many times will that happen again in life? Don't get back home only to realize that you stayed in your cabin too much and didn't savor every part of the trip.

Nellie Kelly

Nellie Kelly is a 24 year old journalist living in Tulsa, Oklahoma. She was born in Tupelo, Mississippi, also the birthplace of Elvis Presley. Her link to Elvis was her only claim to fame until she took a freighter to South America in 1995.

After the trip, she graduated from The University of Southern Mississippi in Hattiesburg. She now writes feature stories at the Tulsa World, *a newspaper in Tulsa, Oklahoma. She shares an apartment with her two ferrets.*

Serendipity

Jackie views every trip as an adventure after her travels to the Antarctic.

by Jackie Smith

I remember taking a walk with my mom around a lake near my aunt's house in Virginia when I was very young. We had been in the car all day traveling from Georgia to Virginia so we were taking this time to stretch our legs. We came across an area near the lake totally taken over by wild blackberry bushes. We filled our pockets and made pouches out of our shirts to collect all the blackberries we could. When we returned to my aunt's house we all joined together in the kitchen to make wild blackberry cobbler. As we finished our delicious cobbler, my mom explained the word "serendipity" to me. Serendipity, she said, was finding something that you weren't even looking for. So by taking a walk, we found the blackberries, made the cobbler, and formed a memory of my mom, my family, and my childhood that I'll never forget.

One Tuesday during fall quarter of 1995, I went to my oceanography class just like I always did on Tuesday and Thursday mornings. My professor had not prepared a lecture for that day, but instead, used the class time to share his slides of his trip to Antarctica. He had taken four students to

Antarctica during Christmas break the previous year. I was captivated by his slides of the icebergs, penguins, seals, mountains, and all the other sights Antarctica had to offer. I approached my professor after class to see if he had any plans to take more students back to Antarctica. He referred me to Dr. Howard Berna who was leading Mercer University's second trip to Antarctica that would be leaving in four weeks.

I immediately went upstairs to find Dr. Berna. I introduced myself and told him of my interest in joining him on his Antarctic journey. I was afraid it would be too late to join because my professor had said all the plans had been set since last spring. Dr. Bema smiled and said that he had just talked to the travel agency. It seems that the expedition cruise had ended up with one more opening due to someone who had backed out at the last minute. After several phone calls to confirm the opening, I was guaranteed a spot on the expedition. By just going to my class that morning, I had experienced serendipity again.

After that, everything happened so fast that I never had time to really reflect on what I was about to do. The few weeks prior to my trip were filled with ordering supplies, getting a passport, and researching the areas where we would be traveling. Still to this day I stop and think, "Wow, I was at the bottom of the earth! I have traveled to the last untouched, natural paradise!" It still seems like a dream.

We left the Atlanta airport on my 21st birthday, December 10, 1995. We traveled from Atlanta to Miami, to Santiago, Chile, and finally to Ushuaia, Argentina. In Ushuaia we boarded our boat, *Professor Multanovskiy*, and set sail for the Antarctic.

Our boat held about 50 crew members and 40 passengers. The boat was a Russian icebreaker. The captain and his crew were all Russian, but a Canadian company owned the boat and the boat manager and expedition leaders were all Canadian. There were also two scientists from England on board. The passengers were English, American, and Canadian. The attitude among the passengers surprised me greatly. There was my group, Dr. Berna and his five students, who were there for the learning experience. Then there were others who seemed to just want another stamp in their passport. It was a very culturally diverse group, which I felt added to the excitement.

We sailed for two days through what is known as Drake Passage. This was probably the most adventurous leg of the trip. "The Drake," as we affectionately referred to it, is where the cool waters of the Atlantic meet the warmer waters of the Pacific, thus, making it the wildest most unpredictable waters in the world. If one is prone to seasickness, The Drake is a nightmare; even if one is not prone to seasickness, The Drake is still pretty menacing. There were probably about two thirds of the passengers whom I never saw until we made it through The Drake. They simply could not get out of their beds for those two days.

In fact, I ended up with numerous bruises from these days across The Drake; I often felt like the pinball in a pinball game while walking around the boat. When I would lie in my bed and look out the porthole, I wouldn't see a horizon. I would see all sky, then all sea, and then all sky again. I was very thankful for my strong stomach.

During our sail from South America to Antarctica, those of us who ventured out of our rooms would hang around in the deck area to watch the graceful wandering albatross circle our ship or watch the horizon hoping to see a whale breach the surface. We saw countless numbers of petrels (a type of sea bird), albatross, and other birds. We saw humpback whales, minke whales, and unidentified whale sprays. I saw my first iceberg and then saw hundreds more throughout the trip. It was truly magical to see the pictures from the books I had read prior to my trip come alive before me.

We lived on the boat and would travel to various landing sites around the Antarctic Peninsula. We traveled on Zodiac Cruisers from our boat to the mainland. We bundled up in layers of polypropylene liners, polar fleece, and Gore-Tex to prepare for our first landings. The most important thing in Antarctica is to remain dry. Many times when getting off the

Zodiacs, we had to stand in knee deep water. Proper attire to remain dry was a must.

On day three of our voyage, I first stepped foot on Antarctica. It was a feeling unlike any other. Adelie penguins and elephant seals greeted us as we unloaded from the Zodiacs. The penguins bobbed along like toddlers first learning to walk. The elephant seals roared, burped, and challenged each other noisily to battles for domination of the pack. I would often find a rock somewhere out of the way and just sit and observe this new world around me.

Each landing offered much of the same. There were always penguins, seals, and exotic birds. Sometimes we would visit the research stations. A few times we saw old abandoned whaling camps that would be littered with massive whalebones. No matter the site, no matter what it had to offer, it never got old. I couldn't see too much of any of it.

In between landings, we would attend lectures on the boat. The boat's professors as well as our own Dr. Berna gave these lectures, however, my favorite activity was joining my classmates and new friends in the ship's bar called The Blowhole, for a recap of what the day had offered. The expedition leaders would join us here and tell us of their years of travel in the Arctic and Antarctic.

After five days in the Antarctic, we pulled back up to port in Argentina. Never had I dreaded the end of a trip the way I dreaded this one. I was half hoping that the crew had decided all of a sudden that they needed a 21-year-old, red-headed college student on board for the rest of the season to perform odd jobs. But like all adventures, this one had to end. But a spark for adventure was lit in me that to this day has not subsided. Whether I'm traveling up to North Carolina for a weekend of backpacking or traveling to Denmark to study for the summer, I now view all of my travels as adventures. Actually, I view life as an adventure.

We just need to open our eyes to those adventures before us. Like Helen Keller said, "Life is either a daring adventure or nothing at all."

Jackie Smith

Jacqueline Maria Smith (Jackie), born on December 10, 1974, is the second and youngest daughter of Charles and Lynn Smith who own a local business in Newman, Georgia. Charlie is also the vice president of a local bank and Lynn serves on the state legislature as a Representative for her district.

While growing up in Newman, Jackie enjoyed playing sports and exploring her interests in math and science. Each season, Jackie was the only girl in her soccer and baseball little leagues. She also competed in tennis and eventually received a tennis scholarship at her university. Jackie discovered her love of math and science in high school when she worked for the Georgia Youth Science and Technology Center.

She pursued her interests in math and science at Mercer University's School of Engineering where she graduated in Environmental Engineering in May of 1998. At the university, Jackie grew to accept every challenge that came her way. Through Mercer she has traveled to Chile, Argentina, Antarctica, Sweden, and Denmark.

Jackie hopes to move to North Carolina to work as an environmental consultant. Her lifelong goal is to travel to every continent before her 40th birthday. She would like to encourage everyone to be open minded and willing to accept the new adventures traveling can offer.

A Challenge in Calcutta

Working with Mother Teresa in Calcutta gave Jessica a new outlook on fear.

by Jessica Davey

"Why did I choose to come here?" As I walked through the streets of Calcutta on the eve of the summer monsoons with beggars and street children jostling against the heat to reach for me, I could not help but wonder, "Is this really what I dreamed of doing?"

My adventure in India began when I was seven years old and saw a T.V. documentary about Mother Teresa. I was fascinated by her work and announced to my family that one day I would travel to the Calcutta of Mother Teresa. I learned more about this Catholic nun through books and periodicals. I wrote letters and posted drawings to "Mother," the other sisters, and the children in the orphanages. A Mason jar in our kitchen collected pennies, dimes, and dollar bills from my baby-sitting jobs. Eventually that money became the savings account for which I had great plans.

In 1992, my childhood dream began to emerge as a reality. I received a letter from Mother Teresa inviting me to "come and serve the poorest of the poor on the streets of Calcutta." In May 1993, I boarded British Airways Flight 143 bound for India with the financial support of the Mary Reynolds Babcock Foundation, Wake Forest University, and the moral support of my family and friends. Suddenly, however, the years of dreaming and planning seemed inadequate preparation for the challenge that greeted me in Calcutta.

In my journal, I documented the steps I took to prepare for my journey. I reflected on any reading and paid particular attention to my own feelings and emotions surrounding this adventure. The most meaningful of my preparatory reflections was a list of fears. That list of fears expanded and changed throughout my adventure. One of the most powerful lessons I learned in Calcutta was that fear is real, no matter how trivial or insignificant it may seem. The experience of being afraid is always real. I was gripped by visceral, heart-pounding fear on occasion during my adventure, yet I came to know the experience as normal and healthy. Realizing that fear is nothing to be ashamed of and can be overcome was an empowering lesson for me. I learned this lesson from the sisters who work tirelessly in extreme conditions, from the volunteers, most of whom share the common experience of culture shock, and from the people whose daily existence has long been defined by fear. I also learned from myself.

I set off for India to learn deep truths and seek hard-won answers to life's great questions. I was a student ready to be guided by a teacher; ready to sit at the feet of Mother Teresa, a sage and humble leader. Rather ironically, it was from within myself–through my reflections, my reactions, and choices–that I learned the deepest truths and the most meaningful lessons.

Each day in Calcutta was its own adventure. Calcutta is a city of seventeen million people, at least two million of whom lie on the pavements and the streets. Walking down the sidewalk was a bit like being a chrome ball plunking through a pinball machine. The daily commute to work was like playing a childhood game of sardines on steamy summer nights when you hold your breath to make room for just one more person.

I lived in a small flat (apartment) in the Muslim Quarter.

Four other young women and I shared two bedrooms, a bath with an erratic water supply, and an area for preparing food. We visited the communal pump like local women for water during the Monsoon. We witnessed the colorful Muslim festivals, observed the cultural and religious traditions of our neighbors, and participated in the daily life of the community.

My favorite part of our daily ritual was the walk to Mother House at dawn. Before the sun even rubbed their eyes, women had started already cooking fires on the curbs. Curls of steam rose out of steel pots of boiling milk tea. The sounds of metal buckets clanking against the pavement, vigorous scrubbing, and the whoosh-whoosh suctioning of the water pumps as people took their morning baths in the dark all made for a dependable alarm clock. By the time we reached Mother House, the head-quarters of Mother Teresa's order of the Missionaries of Charity, the sun had risen, baths were complete, and the chai (milk tea) consumed.

Mass started at 5:45 am. In tidy rows the sisters, clad in simple white saris with blue stripes, sat on the floor reciting the daily meditations. In the rear corner of the chapel, Mother knelt each morning with the volunteers, young and old, from all over the world. After mass and breakfast (bread, banana, and chai), we all dispersed to various homes for the morning. Mother Teresa operated over a dozen homes for the infirm, the dying, the orphaned, and the handicapped in Calcutta alone. Over my three months in Calcutta, I worked in most of them, although most days, I worked at Prem Dan, a home for 350 mentally and physically handicapped adults, Shishu Bhavan, the orphanage, and Kalighat, Mother Teresa's original home for the dying.

Much of the work was labor intensive–pulling water from the wells for baths and laundry, bathing the patients, scrubbing the wards, and washing the clothes and linen. When we were not busy with chores, we had time to sit with patients, talk or sing, or simply touch or massage them. The moments that remain most vivid in my memory are the times I sat with patients as they died. The gentle quiet of human touch, the peace of kind words and prayers as a patient died, and then the busyness of washing and shrouding the body, afterwards, touched me very deeply. The commonplace nature of and the familiarity with death that the sisters, patients, and Indian culture demonstrated were challenging, yet somehow very comforting.

One morning I arrived at Mother House ready for another day at Prem Dan. Volunteers quickly carved out a niche in the routine; I looked forward to laundry each day–the squishing, the beating, the stomping, and especially the singing–as we all, sisters and volunteers, stooped shoulder to shoulder around the cement tub. This day, however, the sister in charge of volunteers instructed me to go to Titaghar, a leprosy center north of Calcutta. In my arms I carried some textbooks, in my sweaty palms, a scrap of paper with a train number scrawled in gloppy blue ink, and in my chest, fear. It was my second week in Calcutta, and I had to navigate my way through Sealdah Railway Station, a place I associated with grim, historical black and white images of massacred Indians and lines of refugees during the Partition of 1947. My destination loomed vague, overwhelming, defined only by stereotypes about lepers and their illness.

Prior to my departure for India, I could articulate at least three fears very specifically: the fear of being alone, the fear of being sick, and the fear of touching a leper. It was not until the end of my first day at Titaghar that my personal space and my boundary of safety was truly challenged. As I toured the wards, I greeted the patients in the Indian tradition of bowing to one another–a gesture that requires no physical contact. Impressed as I was by the efficiency and the accomplishments of the center as well as touched by the joyful people who call Titaghar home, I was still anxious to leave, even if it meant getting back on a packed train.

Right at the door, however, a man with knubby fingers and a scarred face reached for my hands and touched them to his own head, a sacred part of the body in Eastern cultures. "Thank you," he said. This exchange represented a touchstone for me. Suddenly I was aware of the abject isolation that a leper experiences. I remembered the utter loneliness I felt when I first arrived in Calcutta, and how moved I had been because of the deepest poverty that exists. Mother Teresa taught me that the most devastating poverty is the poverty of abandonment–of being alone and being no one to anyone. Because of a kind spirit in the bald and shriveled body of a leper, I understood this lesson.

There are many memories. Some memories are simple images. Others are complicated stories that serve as testaments to what I learned, and help record how I changed. There are even more people who were both teachers and fellow classmates. While none of my family and friends made this first trip with me, they were indeed sojourners without whom I could not have walked down the jetway to board my flight. My source of courage was undoubtedly my family because they believed long before I did that I could do anything; they demonstrated this by supporting me, encouraging me in the face of obstacles, and by providing me space and time to make my own decision without fear of disappointing them. During my first and longest nights in Calcutta, that knowledge and my faith sustained me. I often thought of Mother Teresa, who set off by steamship for India at the age of eighteen. I tried to imagine what her list of fears might have included or what she felt when she first disembarked at Calcutta. It was the concrete and tangible influence of fellow volunteers, however, that convinced me I really was meant to be in Calcutta and that I had a purpose to fulfill in being there.

In some ways it is challenging to write about this one experience as "my adventure." I believe that the spirit of adventure is compromised by isolating it or limiting it to an event, a place, or one experience. The truths I discovered, the lessons I continue to learn, and the strength I found within myself are a part of my daily life. Much of what I have gleaned from this experience has been in the reflection and sharing that I have done following my return from Calcutta. There is so much more to an adventure than a single event, accomplishment, product, or destination. What one chooses to do with new knowledge, insights, and experience is another part of one's adventure. An adventure never ends. My advice to any adventurer is to be mindful that each step and each choice is an integral part of the adventure. If so, adventure boldly; you will never be finished!

Jessica Davey

"Passion" is Jessica Davey's secret to a successful life, and is the word she chooses to describe herself. Born April 12, 1973, Jessica discovered her passion at an early age through community service and believes her life has been directed by her desire to serve others. Jessica's interest in serving oth-ers began within her own family, when her family provided foster care for infants awaiting adoption.

Jessica further developed her interest in helping others by volunteering through her school and church in Norfolk, Virginia. As a high school student, Jessica volunteered with Operation Smile International and the local Children's Hospital. Her commitment to service gained an international perspective when she volunteered in West Africa and the Middle East. While attending Wake Forest University as a Presidential Scholar for Community Service and Leadership, Jessica worked as a volunteer with the homeless, the elderly, and with students in area schools.

These experiences helped Jessica pursue her childhood dream of working with Mother Teresa in Calcutta, India, which she describes as her greatest adventure yet! "The key to adven-turing is not much different from the secret to life," says Jessica. "One must be passionate; passionate about living, learning, and growing. One must treasure each step in the process as its own adventure. True adventures, like life, are not merely destinations, but journeys."

Studying Lemurs in Madagascar

Becca makes managerial decisions in an African rain forest.

by Becca Lewis

After an overnight flight from Nairobi, Kenya, I was tired. I had not been able to sleep much on the plane but my adrenaline was keeping me going. I had just landed in Madagascar to research wild lemurs in a rain forest. I had worked with captive lemurs at the Duke University Primate Center in North Carolina, but this experience would be much more intense. I was headed for a remote research site without electricity or running water and had no idea what to expect. I knew that I could do it, though; I had just spent three months backpacking on the mainland of East Africa, an experience that would prove to be good preparation.

I had just completed college with a degree in biological anthropology. I wanted to see the world. Africa and the cultures of its peoples had always called to me. I decided to travel in East Africa and secured a position as a research assistant in Madagascar to round out the year.

In preparation for the trip, I took a Swahili class. It was quite useful while I backpacked and it even allowed me to travel alone to areas where tourists generally do not go. As I entered Madagascar, however, I was amazed at how few people speak English; I wished that I had studied French as well as Swahili.

I was in Madagascar to assist Joyce Powzyk, a primatologist (a person who studies monkeys and other primates). Although I had conversed with her on the phone, I had never met her. My biggest fear was not that something terrible was going to happen to me in the forest or that I would hate the hard work, but that I would not get along with the one person with whom I would be able to converse in camp.

Would she like me? Would I like her?

Joyce had been unable to meet me in town and had sent Ndrina, the head guide, to bring me into camp. The camp site was 23 kilometers from Andasibe in Mantady National Park. The hike was hot and difficult. I was in pretty good shape but began to question whether I was suited for the work in these mountains. The path climbed the mountain at a very steep rate, and Ndrina always seemed to be waiting for me as I dragged along.

Camp was unlike many research sites. We had only one permanent structure–a kitchen area composed of a fire pit and a few hand-crafted seats, sheltered from the rain by a thatched roof held up by homemade poles. Also in camp were Joyce's tent, my tent, a tent for the two guides (Ndrina and Marcel), and a latrine. This area of the rain forest was old growth and pristine. Therefore, we did our best to keep an environmentally sound camp. Food was hiked in twice a month, and all the trash was hiked out. We drank directly from the stream. To keep the water clean we used biodegradable soap, and bathed from a bucket away from the stream to avoid contamination. We were visitors in the forest, and thus, tried to minimize our impact.

My biggest fear quickly passed as soon as I met Joyce. We became instant friends. The guides, however, decided to test me on my first night by bringing a local "delicacy"–palm larva! I am a vegetarian and normally refuse to eat animals. But this occasion was not one I refused. I needed to show that I was not squeamish, but strong; besides, I had never had larva before. They were good and tasted just like popcorn; I even had seconds!

We were studying two types of lemurs–the diademed sifaka and the indri. These two species are closely related and live in the same area of the forest. Joyce wanted to know how they could live together without competing for the same food sources. The work and the terrain were extremely difficult. We awoke every morning at four, prepared a breakfast of beans and rice, and hiked into the forest to find the study group for the day's research. We had to get up early enough to find the lemurs in their sleep trees so we could record their behavior from the moment they awoke until they went to bed. After a full day of running up and down the mountains trying to follow them and record everything they did in a day, we would hike back to camp at five or six in the evening to cook another meal of rice and beans and go to bed so that we could do it all again the next day.

I grew accustomed to my new life quickly, but it was very different from living in civilization. I did not have a mirror and started to forget how I looked. I had adverse reactions to my anti-malarial drugs; each weekly dose would give me the shakes and crazy, vivid nightmares. I began to question my identity; every adjective I used to define myself was irrelevant in the forest. The ground seemed to be slipping out from underneath me.

This unstable time passed. I quit taking the anti-malarial drugs and used other preventive methods. I learned to define myself from within. I learned to speak French with the guides, and we soon became friends. We told stories while drinking tea and roasting peanuts over the campfire. This was my life in camp. It seemed so normal. I could hardly remember my life any other way.

Ten weeks after I had entered the forest, Joyce returned to the U.S. to begin analyzing her data. We had discussed this, but it had not occurred to me that when she left, I would be the one who had to run the camp. Collecting the behavioral data had become routine for me, but I had not considered the many other responsibilities.

I had learned to identify the genus and sometimes the species of close to 200 plants. I had helped Joyce collect phenological data and weigh, dry, and pack plant samples to be returned to the U.S. for nutritional analysis. Now I was responsible for planning the daily schedule, provisioning camp so that we could eat, paying salaries, and writing reports for local and national officials. Because the guides did not speak English, business was all conducted in French and Malagasy.

For the most part, camp continued as before. I was young but not entirely inexperienced. I had learned to manage people while I directed the Connecticut office of Green Corps, an environmental group, when I was twenty. I had to draw on cultural sensitivity refined during my travels. I had to learn to speak some Malagasy and improve my French. My position in camp and in the local village changed, too. I was no longer Joyce's assistant; I was the boss and the wage payer. People began to beg for work and for money. Being a young, unmarried woman also presented problems. Very few women in Madagascar held leadership positions much less supervised men who were older than they. It was difficult for the guides and the townspeople to accept me as the boss.

Holidays came and passed. I spent them alone. The guides were in town with their families. I had my letters from friends and family. I had a Christmas stocking, stuffed weeks before with a treasured candy bar. I had the call of the indri to keep me company.

New Year's Day I slept late, only to be awakened by strangers in camp. Two men walked near my tent as I rushed to dress. It was the local playboy who had been trying to win my affection in town, carrying a picnic lunch to share with me. One of our porters had shown him the way. I was furious. No one was to be allowed in camp without permission. He was definitely not invited, nor did I want to be alone with a strange man miles from town. Thinking quickly, I asked if he had a government permit to be in the national park. He looked puzzled as he replied, "No." I informed him that he was trespassing and that

I would have him arrested if he did not leave the park immediately. After standing firm and repeating my position, he returned to town.

In those two weeks that I was alone during the holidays, I experienced another instance with trespassers. I kept seeing footprints along our trails. I followed them daily, half-crazed with anger that someone would dare be in "my" forest and half-scared that I would find whoever it was. My only protection was my wits. I tracked the footprints for days but found no one. Ndrina came into camp a few days early to make sure that supplies had lasted. I asked him if he thought that I was in danger. He was flabbergasted. He could not understand why I was afraid. I asked if the person might have a gun. He could not fathom why I thought that just anyone would have a gun; only Malagasy police and military had guns. I asked if I, being a woman, had reason to fear being assaulted. Again, these fears were not relevant here. Ndrina did find a small camp of people living nearby. They were after food that could be extracted from the forest. Inflation was making it difficult for people to afford food in town. They were more afraid of me than I was of them.

In March I received notice that my visa could not be renewed. I had to be on the next flight out of the country, five days later. I had not yet finished the research and had no way to contact Joyce. I sent the guides into town to gather porters to help carry everything out of the forest. As the last researcher to leave, I had to return the forest to its undisturbed state. Six months after I had entered the forest, I left. The forest did not seem to notice that I was leaving, just like it had not noticed my arrival. It simply continued.

I was late reaching the capital. I had time to catch my flight but not enough time to secure the permits needed to transport plants out of the country. Joyce's research depended upon these plants. I locked them in my bag and took a chance. When going through customs, I recalled my drama lessons and pretended to be an inexperienced tourist. I tried to annoy the agent sufficiently so that he would not waste time with me. I was nearly caught–but it worked.

After a month of relaxation in Kenya, I returned to the U.S. safely with Joyce's data, samples, and supplies. Now a new journey began–readjustment to the culture of my own country.

Becca Lewis

Becca was born in California on June 17, 1972, to Joan and Norman Lewis. Debbie, her sister, is three years older. After living in Texas for seven years, the family moved to Pascagoula, Mississippi.

At the age of five, Becca loved to watch nature shows on television and decided she wanted to study apes. In high school, she wanted a career in law and politics, but eventually returned to her original love of primates while studying anthropology at Duke University.

Becca was a leader in her school and the community from the time she was little. In high school, she was president of the student council and was valedictorian of her class. In college, Becca was a gymnastics instructor, community activist, and executive vice president of the student body. In 1993, she directed the Connecticut Office of Green Corps, an environmental organization. She is currently pursuing a doctorate in biological anthropology and anatomy at Duke University.

Field Expedition in the Arctic

Natalia practices field work
under variable weather conditions
in the Arctic.

by Natalia Rybczynski

This is the story of my first trip to the High Arctic. It represents a time of great learning for me. I am happy for the opportunity to tell you this story and I am hoping that you will find something useful in it as you pursue your own adventures.

You never know how an adventure might begin. Although I did not go to the High Arctic until 1994, the root of my adventure lay in the fall of 1987. At this time I was a student at Gloucester High School. I had just signed up to participate in the Mentorship Program. I had indicated that I was interested in paleontology and was matched with Dr. Harington, who was head of the Paleobiology Division at the Canadian Museum of Nature.

I worked that year with Dr. Harington on a restoration of an Ice Age horse, *Equus lambei*. In some respects, the work was tedious. I had to spend hours measuring hundreds of bones, but it was also very rewarding. Over the next several years, I worked with Dr. Harington on several other projects. The time

I spent at the museum left me with the deep impression that field work is one of the most important and enjoyable aspects of paleontology. Part of what drove me to pursue paleontological research was the lure of working in wilderness areas, particularly the Arctic.

At Carlton University (Ottawa), I began running regularly. A large part of my motivation was to be in good physical condition for field work; although at the time, I did not know when the opportunity to do field work might arise. A couple of years later, I joined the cross-country ski team. Besides giving me strength and endurance, this taught me to work hard under difficult conditions and gave me travel experience.

There were no vertebrate paleontologists at Carlton University, so my introduction to fieldwork was through geology, micropaleontology and paleoentomology (fossil insects). In the middle of my last year at Carlton, Dr. Harington offered me a position on a field expedition to the High Arctic.

I felt like I had prepared for this moment my whole life. I was both ecstatic and terrified. Part of my fear was due to the fact that none of my field experiences to date had involved camping. In fact, I had never camped for more than a couple of days at a time! The Arctic trip involved three weeks of camping in entirely isolated conditions. In addition, to go to the Arctic, I was required to get my Firearms Acquisition Certificate (FAC) in case of a polar bear attack. To get an FAC, I had to take a short course and pass a written and practical test. My attitude toward guns up until that point had been very negative. My parents had been strictly against any sort of toy guns in the house as I was growing up. But, a few months later, my mind was changed. By the time I left for the Arctic, not only did I not mind handling guns, but I had joined a local biathlon (shooting and skiing) team.

On July 5, 1994, Dr. Harington, John Tenor, Clayton Kennedy, and I left Ottawa for the Arctic Islands. We took an airline jet to Resolute (Cornwallis Island). Resolute harbors a small native community, as well as a Polar Continental Shelf

Project research station. From Resolute we were flown in a tiny Twin Otter plane to Ellesmere Island. The view from the plane was spectacular. The hills were bare of vegetation but rich in the form and color of their rocks.

The Twin Otter landed on the beach of Strathcona Fiord and the gear was unloaded. As the plane flew away, I felt a twinge of anxiety and isolation. Had I forgotten my toothbrush? But there was no time to worry. We set up camp near the water's edge. An igloo-style cook tent was put in the center of the camp, surrounded by several individual tents. Our work at the site began the next day.

The site is a preserved 3.5 million year old peat bog. Each day we made a strenuous 1,000 foot climb to locality that was made even more challenging by the loose rock and threat of mud slides. From the site we could see the U-shaped valley bottom, a terminal moraine, a lake, and a glacier in the distance. Working through the peat using trowels and our hands, we recovered bones, insects, and numerous pieces of beaver-cut wood, perhaps representing the remains of a dam. Extinct animals such as rabbits, horses, deer, bear and beaver were represented at the site. Their bones were usually dark colored, nearly black, and were often highlighted in blue by the mineral vivianite.

Working conditions varied tremendously. Some days were calm, sunny, and warm. Occasionally we could even wear short sleeved shirts. On other days, blasting winds would wear on our bodies, chill our limbs, and make our eyes muddy. Storms in the high Arctic usually involve little precipitation but very high winds. Often we would have to leave the site early because of the winds or threat of rain.

Even small amounts of rain could be very dangerous. When wet, the terrain became slippery with mud, and climbing up or down the mountainside was nearly impossible. Even walking over the valley bottom was treacherous. Such conditions could keep us camp-bound for days at a time.

On our days off, when the weather was good, we would explore the splendors of the valley. The valley was full of geese, caribou, musk ox, arctic hare, foxes, weasels, and numerous birds. It was also laden with historical artifacts. We visited tent rings, hare traps, and cairns (piles of stones put there by some-one as trail markers) that were supposedly at least 600 years old and attributed to the Thule people. There were also the remains of fossil forests that were perhaps 30 million years old. The wood was brightly colored in yellow and rusts and stood out against the sandy color sediment of the hills. Sometimes I would hike alone. Navigating the area forced me to practice using my spatial memory, and, at times, to be guided by my intuition. Many hikes were graced by the midnight sun, because in the artic at certain times of the year, the sun doesn't set.

On one particularly long hike, Clayton and I found a nar-row, V-shaped valley opening that was being guarded by a lone arctic hare. We left the wind-blasted U-valley, passed the hare and found ourselves walking in absolute stillness up a living bog. The thick mosses were green, red, and orange. We could hear the sound of water trickling below our feet. Small white feathers littered the ground. We took many pictures, but none turned out. I learned that taking pictures cannot be equated with creating memories.

I also learned of the more dangerous and unpredictable aspects of the Arctic. July 11th was the day the great storm began. The temperature had dropped to near freezing and the wind had picked up. By that afternoon the sea-ice had been shoved up onto the shore and crushed our toilet facilities (a bucket). At about 11:30 at night we were awakened by the sound of breaking metal over the screaming winds. The ice had overrun and crushed the cook tent! All of our food and com-munication equipment were at risk. With the ice still moving occasionally, every effort was made to pull out all that we could from under it.

Afterwards, I slept little, for fear that the ice would reach my tent. High winds made it impossible to relocate the tents. The next morning the ice had moved just a yard more. Dr. Harington made a pass by my tent and dropped off a package of roasted almonds and a candy bar. He told me to stay in my tent until noon. By the end of the second day of the storm we had salvaged the cook tent, and had recovered the radio and a large portion of the food. The effect of the ice covering the shoreline was incredible. Ice was piled at least three meters high in places. In other places, it had been pushed forward some 10 to 20 meters inland. On July 13th, a Twin Otter from Resolute dropped off some supplies to replace what we had lost.

Summer in the High Arctic lasts only a few weeks. When we had arrived, the spring flowers were blooming. By the end of the trip it was fall; the flowers were nearly all gone and the leaves of the tiny ground-hugging willow trees had turned to bright orange and yellow. In the distance, wind blasted snow covered the hills. On July 25th, a Twin Otter came from Resolute to pick us up. I cried as the plane lifted out of the valley and turned south through an Arctic storm.

Since then I have participated in several field seasons in the badlands of Alberta, and in July, 1997, I was able to return for the last field season at Strathcona Fiord. Today, I am using material from the Strathcona Fiord locality in my Ph.D. research, and I am making plans to return to the Arctic.

Because of the way I was raised, I never viewed opportunity as gender specific. My advice to others is to never pass up any opportunities that might lead to your dream. Every experience has value, even if you don't recognize it at the time.

Natalia Rybczynski

Natalia was born in Edmonton (Alberta) on November 28, 1971. Nine months later, she and her family moved to Ottawa (Ontario). Her parents, Tony and Galina, provided her with a nurturing environment in which to grow up. She was soon joined by a sparkling little sister, Nina. Unlike her little sister, Natalia often did not appreciate school in her early years. She much preferred talking to the animals, drawing, painting, and playing soccer. She also enjoyed collecting natural objects such as feathers, fossils, and skulls.

In 1994, she graduated with a B.S. from Carlton University (Ottawa), having majored in Biology, Anthropology, and Geology. A thesis on a mammal-like reptile earned her a master of science degree at the University of Toronto in 1996. During this time she also succeeded in making the Ontario biathlon team. She is presently at Duke University completing a doctorate in paleontology.

Adventuring in the Amazon

*Mary Anne's search for birds leads her deep
into other adventures.*

by Mary Anne Peine

As the pickup truck barreled down the deserted, dusty road,
I tried to keep thoughts of "What have we gotten ourselves
into?" at bay by concentrating on the birds. We rode in the back
of a pickup truck, seated on two-by-fours perched on scaffolding just above the cab. The sun was brutal. The cheap pink sunglasses I had bought in the market that morning were all that
protected my eyes from the relentless clouds of dust that bat-
tered my face. My arms were beginning to ache from their tight
grip on the metal scaffolding around my head. I squinted my
eyes and tried to concentrate on the birds.

Eight months in Latin America had turned me into quite the
birdwatcher. It had all started innocently, with a picture of a
macaw on the cover of an old copy of *National Geographic.* My
friend Rachel and I had read the article while visiting a small town
in Ecuador. The descriptions of vast, virgin jungles and rare, beautiful, intelligent, and brightly colored birds were enough to lure us
to Manu National Park in Peru. Before we made it to the park as
tourists, however, we became friends with two Canadian biolo-
gists who gave us the telephone number of the man who had actu-

ally written the *National Geographic* article, Dr. Charlie Munn. When we arrived in Lima two months later, we called Dr. Munn on a whim. To our thrilled, nervous amazement, he called us back and immediately began outlining a plan for us to join him on a research expedition less than a week later. We dropped everything and caught the next flight to Cusco, Peru.

We spent the next two weeks in the Amazon jungle. The first few days were a whirlwind as we realized that we had accidentally stumbled into the company of some of the most influential conservationists in the entire nation of Peru. Rachel and I were introduced to two guides, Pocho and Andres, and a Canadian bird veterinarian named Kent. We spent the next ten days with these three men. In a small boat, we traveled for two days to a remote area of the Heath River on the border of Peru and Bolivia. Our scientific duty was to count macaws at two colpas, or clay licks. The macaws ate the clay to counter the effects of toxic seeds that were a major part of their diet.

Our personal duty was to translate Spanish for Kent and refrain from killing him when he told long, tedious stories about animal surgery and made statements like, "Women are oppressed because they're keeping themselves down and if they truly want equality they have to stop leeching off of men," or "In a marriage, whomever makes more money has a proportional right to make more of the decisions, which is why I'm looking for a woman who makes as much money as I do and won't leech off me." We were successful on all counts.

We also became close friends with Pocho and Andres. Pocho knew birds; Andres drove the boat. Pocho was stout, jovial, and outgoing; Andres was thin, quiet, and friendly. The accumulated wisdom of the two men was overwhelming. Pocho had been a poacher of macaws for the pet trade until Charlie (as Dr. Munn was known to most) began paying him to protect these rare populations of birds. Andres, who proudly stated his profession as "ecologisto" when we crossed the border, had spent over a year on foot exploring the banks of this jungle river for Charlie, locating populations of macaws, river otters, and other species of interest. They put up with our inexperience and our bad campfire cooking because we were funny and rugged, we didn't complain, and we loved the birds.

When we finally returned to Cusco, we were told that Pocho was planning a trip to his hometown of Trinidad, Bolivia. During our time together on the Heath River, Pocho repeatedly tempered our awe and excitement with stories of Trinidad, which he said was the most beautiful town on the face of the earth. Every unbelievable bird we saw was nothing compared to the birds in Trinidad. The landscape was nothing compared to the pampas in Trinidad. The water, the food, the air, the women–they were all better in Trinidad. He promised to show us the time of our lives if we ever visited his hometown. So when we learned that Pocho was planning to go back to Trinidad, we left him a note in Cusco and let the lucky wave of spontaneity carry us to Bolivia.

After a few days of wandering and misadventures by ourselves in Trinidad, Pocho arrived. Twenty-four hours later we were in the back of a pickup truck on the way to see the pampas. My face, lips, arms, hair, and clothes were caked with the stinging sand grains that pelted us as we roared into the pampas. The sheer quantity and variety of birds on either side of the road was enough to make me forget the sun and the dust clouds and even lift my sunglasses once in a while to get a better look. Roseate spoonbills were striking in their brilliant splendor of bright pink feathers. Giant storks seemed disproportionate and impossibly enormous. Toucans lifted the weight of their beaks across the sky. They were all beautiful, but we were here to see just one. We had come to Trinidad to see the blue-throated macaw. There were only 200 to 300 of these macaws left in the wild, and Pocho was one of the only people in the world who knew where they were. He had once been one of the greatest threats to these birds. Now, he was one of their only protectors and he was taking us to see them.

After three hours without a sign of human life, the truck stopped and Pocho motioned Rachel and me to step down. As the truck drove away, leaving us by the side of the road, I thought of all the times I had seen local people step off of buses in the countryside without a house, building, or barn in sight. As I traveled from one town to another, I would wonder where these people were going. Now I was one of those people, but I did not know where I was. As we sat by the side of the road waiting for another truck, I began to fathom just how much trust we had placed in this one man.

The truck never arrived. So we put on our backpacks and started walking down a small side road. After about thirty minutes a truck passed but did not stop. Apparently, this was not the truck the driver said he would send later to pick us up. We sat and watched a beautiful pair of scarlet and black toucans until our truck finally arrived. Late that afternoon, we finally came to our first resting place.

The farmhouse was part of an estancia owned by a wealthy surgeon who lived in town. Four families lived in two houses with dirt floors, tin roofs, and simple plywood walls. Small children ran underfoot everywhere, giggling and hurling high pitched Spanish phrases at each other. The men worked in the fields and the women stayed in the houses all day, working and taking care of the children. They were all extremely friendly, eager to talk without much to say. They watched us eat. They watched us set up our tents. They watched us walk out into the campo in search of a bathroom. Their eyes followed us everywhere we went. One woman, seventeen years old and quite pretty, had just had her first baby. As she held her baby, you could feel the pride and contentment coming off of her in waves–she was the luckiest woman in the world. All of the other children were dirty and afraid of the gringas.

We slept in our tents that night and awoke fairly early the next morning. As we waited for a man to bring horses from an even more remote estancia, the hot, heavy, dead weight of isolation began to press down on us. We waited. We swatted flies, played cards, and tried to explain to Pocho the difference between the English words *bird, bread, bear,* and *beard.* We waited. We wandered around looking for birds. Pocho's sixth sense led us to the giant yellow eyes of a perfectly still, perfectly camouflaged Great Horned Owl. We waited. Finally, a man arrived with three extra horses from La Verde, the second estancia and our final destination. We mounted our horses, backpacks and all, and headed out again into the pampas.

The sun was merciless; sweat poured down my face. The pampas was unlike anything I had seen before. Grasslands stretched out into eternity, an uninterrupted flatness that strained and exhausted my mountain eyes. It looked like my idea of an African savanna. The grass was coarse and grew in tall clumps. The ground was muddy and uneven. I felt sorry for my horse as he trudged through the treacherous expanse. Pocho and our new, unidentified campesino friend yelled at me, ordering me to continually hit my horse with the loose end of the reins in order to speed him up. I felt guilty but the guilt was overcome by the fear of being separated from the only person in the world that knew where we were and would watch out for me–Pocho. I sent a telepathic apology to my horse. I named him Rana, which means frog in Spanish, because when I asked what his name was the two men just laughed at me. Horses don't have names. Why would you name a horse, silly gringa?

The man who led us to La Verde was about thirty years old, quiet and sullen. He whipped his horse constantly and for a while the horse responded. Eventually, the horse refused to go any faster, obviously exhausted.

He fell behind the three of us. Suddenly, Rachel cried out from behind me.

"Mary Anne, I just saw something so horrible. That man took his knife and cut part of his horse's ears off. There's blood everywhere."

I looked back and saw blood pouring down both sides of the horse's face. I turned quickly around again as if I had seen something I shouldn't have seen, as if knowing that I had seen him would cause the man to turn his knife on me. Faced forward in the saddle, rage built pressure behind my eyes and my thoughts swirled in angry reds and blacks. I saw this man beating his horse, beating his wife, beating his children as he fought to establish some sense of control, power, and importance in the face of insurmountable poverty, mind-numbing isolation, and a merciless landscape. I completed the journey to La Verde in silence.

When we finally arrived at La Verde, I was stunned. It seemed as if I had just traveled 100 years back in time and stepped into pioneer America. The house was a simple, ramshackle building with a large, sheltered, open air dining area and a separate kitchen. There were several corrals to one side of the house, a few small shacks, and then the pampas, rolling out into the horizon. Saddles and rank, tanning cow hides were draped over the fences. Pocho told us that there was a road to this house during the four months of the dry season. During the rainy season, the only way to get to the house was by horse or airplane. The surgeon had an airplane. These people, obviously, did not.

The homestead reminded me of countless Appalachian cabins I had seen in the Great Smoky Mountains National Park and the Museum of Appalachia in Norris, Tennessee, as a child. But the Little House on the Prairie romance of these places, conjured up in my head during grade school field trips, evaporated in seconds. Nice ladies in cotton dresses and white bonnets were replaced by an overweight, bored, friendly, silent woman. Young, serious Abe Lincoln and mischievous, good-natured Huck Finn became a group of skittish, dirty, silent, half-wild children. The bountiful promise and possibilities of the new frontier were, in reality, a suffocating sense of isolation and silent resignation. The romance of living with the land was replaced by billions of mosquitoes and a stagnant pool that was the family's main water source. My imagination came face to face with reality–a reality I never dreamed that I would actually see.

After a brief rest, Pocho told us it was time to look for the birds. For some reason, I had thought it would be harder, that we would have to hide in a blind (a camouflage shelter with peepholes) until dusk or wake up before sunrise as we had done on the Heath River. Instead, we simply started listening and walking quietly in the middle of the afternoon. We were in a rather strange ecosystem, made up of only palm trees and nothing on the ground but sand. After the monotony of the pampas, however, this was a blessed relief and I reveled in shade and variety. I sweltered under layers of clothes that kept mosquitoes out and body heat in. We walked. Pocho listened. Suddenly, we all heard the squawking that had become so familiar to Rachel and me on the Heath River, causing an immediate reflex response as we scanned the sky like Pavlov's birdwatchers. But Pocho shook his head.

"No es la grita. La grita de la garganta azul es mas fina. Mas fina. Escucha."

That's not the cry of the blue-throated macaw, he told us. The call of the blue-throated was much finer, much more beautiful. The word *fina* lingered, emphasizing Pocho's reverence for the bird. Several more calls kept us on our toes but it was always a false alarm, another pair of blue and yellow macaws. Pocho had warned us that we might not see the birds at all. He had brought people here before who had gone home without seeing the birds. The birds were so threatened and their numbers were so low that Pocho never knew if he would see any the next time he returned.

Suddenly, Pocho froze in his tracks.

"Escucha," he whispered. Listen.

My memory was filled with the calls of several other macaws and parrots, and I knew immediately that this was completely different from anything I had heard before. Pocho led us toward the sound, moving silently across the sand. As we tiptoed behind him, the heat, the mosquitoes, the estancia, and the pampas dissolved, melting into the periphery. All that existed was the sound of a bird. My mind raced in an incoherent blur that found its only focus in that sound.

Pocho stopped walking. A smile spread across his face. He had found his old friends one more time. He pointed up into a tree less than twenty-five yards away. Rachel and I looked up into the tree and immediately spotted the birds. There were three pairs perched in the tree above us. Macaws mate for life and each bird is very affectionate towards its mate. These birds were no exception, constantly crooning to each other in low voices and preening each other's feathers. Rachel and I passed binoculars back and forth as we crept forward, almost imperceptibly, toward the birds.

If I close my eyes now, I can still see them perfectly–the rich, dusty, cobalt blue back; the stripe of yellow down both sides of the face that spills into the breast; the black and white stripes sweeping back around the eyes; the blue starting beneath the eye and curving under the throat. I watched these birds in quiet reverence, contemplating their peril and why I, of all people, was so fortunate as to glimpse this shadow of their former majesty. As I stood in the shade of the palm trees I began to feel the culmination of so many years rushing towards me from hundreds of directions. All the separate links of my path thus far had conspired to create this moment–hiking in the Great Smoky Mountains National Park every week during the summer as a child; blindly hurling myself into the environmental movement; a long, intimate relationship with the Southern Appalachian mountains; solitary revelations in the deserts of the Southwestern United States; the slow unfolding of my plan to spend a year in Latin America; months of fruitless planning in Tennessee; the fear and blind faith of an open ended plane ticket to Quito, Ecuador; Costa Rica; Rachel; the weariness of danger and diseases and loneliness from months of traveling; finally reaching the Amazon, one of my few specific, concrete dreams; Charlie; Pocho; trucks; horses; the surprising way my dreams play themselves out in reality, like nothing I would have ever expected.

We watched the blue-throated macaws until our eyes and ears were full of them. We returned to the estancia that evening. Rachel and I bathed by pouring water on ourselves from a bucket, sheltered within a flimsy enclosure. In the cool, naked evening breeze, a pair of blue and yellow macaws flew across the brilliant sunset over our heads. The woman of the house prepared dinner, always different variations on the same food–charkey (like the jerkey eaten by hunters, trappers, and settlers of the American West). This dried, intensely salted meat was basically the only thing I ever saw people eat on both of the estancias. Every day, they ate this tough, salty, dried meat with rice or noodles. The only vegetables I ever saw were a few carrots and potatoes that we had brought with us and donated to the cooks. It was an unbelievable diet. I could not believe that they raised children on this food. My digestive system did not know what to do with it. I drank water all the time but never urinated, and my intestines were tied up in knots. But we accepted it all with deep gratitude, a gratitude expressed by eating, by compliments, by sharing our company. The poverty here and the sacrifice made in giving us this meat were unfathomable and definitely indescribable.

That evening, billions of mosquitoes descended on the estancia. The woman who lived there told me that two of her children had allergies to mosquitoes. When they were bitten too many times they would swell up, inside and out, unable to eat, drink, pick anything up, or see. I knew that there were two men on the estancia and they were both married, but I had only seen this woman and so I asked her where the other woman was. She looked at me as if she was a bit confused.

"Right over there," she said, pointing to a girl sitting on a bench beside the wall. I used every ounce of willpower I possessed to hold back my disbelief.

"How old is she?" I asked.

"Fourteen," the woman replied. That would put her in eighth or ninth grade in the U.S. Not only was she married, but she was married to the thirty year old man who had cut off pieces of his horses ears on the ride to the estancia. The realities of these people's lives spun around my head and made me dizzy with disbelief.

That night, the awning of our tent was black with tiny insect bodies as the air pulsed with the eerie hum of billions of mosquitoes. The sound was unlike anything I had ever heard before. If I concentrated on the buzzing, I could hear it extending for miles

113

in every direction, becoming larger and fuller with each passing second. As the humming filled the world and lulled me to sleep, I thought of the lives that had collided with mine and wondered who was going to come home in my body. I had made my pilgrimage to a temple of mosquitoes and crocodiles. My prayers were feathers of blue and yellow. They filled the jungle skies.

Mary Anne Peine

Mary Anne Peine lives in Asheville, North Carolina, where she works as the executive director of the Southern Appalachian Biodiversity Project. The Biodiversity Project is a non-profit environmental advocacy group dedicated to protecting the native ecosystems and wildlife of the Southern Appalachians. She received a Bachelor of Arts in Environmental Science and Policy from the University of Tennessee in 1997. Prior to graduation, she was recognized on the 1997 USA Today College All-Academic Team and received a Chancellor's Citation for Extraordinary Campus Leadership and Service and another for Extraordinary Professional Promise. As a student, she founded the University of Tennessee student environmental group and had papers presented at international environmental conferences.

She grew up in Sevierville, Tennessee, where her love of the outdoors and rapid development in her community led her to become involved with environmental issues at an early age. Her father is a scientist with the U.S. Geological Survey; her mother is an assistant principal and a former teacher of gifted education; and her younger sister is a student at the Evergreen State College in Olympia, Washington, and an adventurer in her own right.

Section II

Planning Your Own Adventures and Challenges

Getting Involved and Taking Action

Now that you've read about girls and young women who have participated in various adventures, you may want to consider your own. An adventure can take a lot of different forms and can be described in many ways. For the purposes of this book we define adventure as any new experience that involves mental and physical preparation.

What does it take to be an adventurer? Let's take a look at a list of characteristics and behaviors of adventurers and compare them to your own.

- Successful adventurers have...
  - Self-Confidence
  - Persistence
  - Ambition
  - A Strong Desire to Achieve
  - Self-Discipline
  - Optimism

- Successful adventurers are...
  - Risk Takers
  - Goal Setters

    – Physically and Mentally Healthy

    – Brave

    – Logical Thinkers

    – Well Prepared

Do some of these traits/behaviors describe you? If so, you are already headed for adventure! If not, identify how you can begin developing yourself in these areas. Understanding your own strengths and limitations will not only help you successfully complete an adventure, but this self knowledge can help you achieve anything you want in life!

You may also want to consider what types of adventures match your interests:

- What are your current hobbies?

- Do you like the outdoors? If so, to what kinds of climates, land forms, and plant life are you attracted?

- What types of sports or cultural activities interest you most?

- What kinds of books and magazines do you find yourself drawn to?

- What kinds of travel do you most enjoy?

- Do you have any collections? If so, could an adventure be designed around adding to your collection?

- How do you most like to spend your time?

- If you could go anywhere in the world, where would it be?

- Are you afraid of heights, water, being alone?

Answering these type questions can help you determine your specific interests and the types of adventures that may be best for you. Certainly you want to plan an adventure that you will ENJOY!

Now that you've examined your personal strengths, limitations, and interests, you may want to consider the benefits of taking an adventure. According to the President's Council on Physical Fitness and Sports, female high school athletes tend to get better grades and are less likely to drop out than their nonathletic counterparts. Also, a study sponsored by the Women's Sports Foundation found that high school girls who play sports are 92 percent less likely than nonathlete girls to be involved with drugs and 80 percent less likely to have an unwanted pregnancy. Read back through the stories of the girls and young women. The adventurers highlighted in this book give you many reasons for pursuing your own adventure. Here are a few to think about:

- Adventures increase your self-confidence and independence.
- Adventures help quench your desire to experience life to its fullest extent.
- Adventures test your limits and lead you to greater self understanding.
- Adventures help lessen your fears.
- Adventures build important life skills in leadership and working with other people.
- Adventures increase your understanding of and appreciation for life and all the beauty it holds.
- Adventures are physically and mentally rewarding.

Now, Let's Get Started with Your Own Adventure!

Positive Risk Taking

Many years ago women who dared to speak out, act bravely, or even *whistle* were considered a threat to society. The cultural expectations for women were conformity, silence, and ladylike behavior at all costs. Today, girls and young women are encouraged to be themselves–to state opinions, ask for what is needed, explore challenges, do something out of the ordinary, and take some risks!

Positive risk taking involves taking the plunge of trying something new when you're not sure whether or not you'll be supported or whether or not you'll even be good at it! Sometimes experiencing the unforeseen or exploring a new groove can be frightening and intimidating. One way you can overcome the fear of taking the risk is to study the risk. What are the benefits of the risk? Do those benefits outweigh the risk involved? What are the outcomes from those who have taken this risk or a similar one before you? Collect this and other information about the risk through your local library, interviews, phone calls, databases, and the internet. Also, another way to reduce your fear of the risk involved is to get some of your friends involved–especially if it's your first adventure. This may help you to feel safer and less intimidated than if you do it alone. The thrill of taking a risk can be exhilarating. In fact, some people are known as thrill seekers or adrenaline junkies. But remember, a well prepared adventurer has carefully calculated the risks involved before jumping into it!

Goal Setting

Goal setting begins with the belief that what you desire is possible. You can set long term goals of what types of adventures you want to take in five, ten, or twenty years from now. You can also set short term goals for adventures you want to do in the immediate future. When determining your goals, be sure to state them very clearly and definitely. Here are examples of vague and clear goal statements:

Vague: *"I want to be a mountain climber."*

Clear: *"I will climb Mt. Everest by July of 2020."*

The more clearly you state the goal and have positive expectations of achieving the goal, the more likely you will accomplish it!

Also, be sure to write down your goals. It may be helpful to keep an *Adventure Journal* as you plan and prepare for your adventure. The journal will be a place you can record all your thoughts, feelings, and actions as you pursue your goals. In addition to the journal, write your goal statement(s) on a type of card that can be placed where you can see it every day. This will serve as a reminder that each day you need to do something that puts you closer to your goal. As Jo Coudert said in the article *How to be a Winner*, "Goals are daydreams unless you work toward them every day."

After your goal has been determined and recorded, you should begin the process of approaching the adventure–from researching and reading about it to planning for it and establishing timelines. The timeline or calendar of activities can be one way of breaking the goal into smaller, more manageable parts. This will make the adventure become more of a reality for you and may motivate you to be disciplined in your pursuit.

121

Physical Preparation

Appropriate physical training is needed to prepare for your adventure. Many of the girls and young women in this book tell of how they prepared themselves for a successful adventure. As a rule, young persons are more habitually active than adults. Young people may experience a higher incidence of overuse injuries if endurance exercise is excessive. The risk of injury can be greatly decreased by ensuring appropriate matching of the activity to your size, maturation and skill level, use of properly fitted protective equipment, and proper conditioning and skill development.

Another concern for youth who exercise is the inability to adapt to thermal stress. Children don't have the sweating capabilities of adults; thus it is more difficult for their bodies to get acclimated or accustomed to heat or cold climatic extremes. In general, children and youth have a lower tolerance time in extreme heat which means you should plan for a longer and more gradual program of acclimatization. Remember to drink plenty of water and other appropriate fluids recommended by your physician.

The following general principles for children and youth are offered by the American College of Sports Medicine to guide you through an appropriate strength training program. But remember, you should always consult your physician before beginning any new exercise program and work with a well trained professional in the exercise field!

- No matter how big and strong you are, your body is physiologically immature.
- Heavy weights can be potentially dangerous and damaging to the developing skeletal and joint structures.
- Limit strength training sessions to twice per week.
- Perform full range multi-joint and multi-muscle exercises. Don't overload any single joint or muscle group.

- Do not overload the joint and skeletal structures with maximal weights.

- All strength training activities should be closely supervised and monitored by appropriately trained personnel.

If you do injure yourself, be sure to see a physician immediately. Usually the first 72 hours after a sports injury, the RICE treatment regimen should be followed–rest, ice, compression, and elevation. Adequate rest and recovery time are also very important in your physical preparation. Although exercising helps you sleep better, make sure your exercise routine ends at least two hours before bedtime.

In addition to physical training, remember other aspects of getting your body prepared. Choosing a healthy diet is critical to your success as an adventurer. You should try to eat nutritious foods in the daily proportions suggested by the USDA Food Guide Pyramid. That means 60 percent of your calories should come from carbohydrates like breads, cereal, rice, and pasta. Make sure you are eating foods that provide your body with vitamins and nutrients. Eating three meals a day is best, but if you can't work that into your schedule, be *sure* to have a good breakfast. Remember that whole grain, low fat foods will give you much more of a boost than empty calories like pastries and doughnuts!

In addition to talking with your physician about your plans for the adventure, you may want to consult with others who have successfully completed similar adventures. Seek out advice through all sources of information in order to get the best information for physical preparation.

Another factor to consider in the physical preparation for an adventure is the selection and use of proper equipment. A motto of successful adventurers is "safety first!" Safety certainly is the key to having the best experience on your adventure. First and foremost you should investigate the type of equipment necessary for the adventure. Really do your research to make sure you get the safest equipment needed. Check with trained professionals to be sure you have your facts straight on the safest gear. The following guidelines are offered to give you an idea of the type of equipment planning necessary:

- Before the trip, determine the specific climate, land forms, animals, insects, or hazards of the area.
- Take a first aid kit with extra supplies for emergencies and first-aid handbook.
- Check all safety equipment to be sure it's in place and working properly.
- Take sunscreen and bug repellent if appropriate for the area.
- Take a compass, matches, flashlight, pocket knife, and first aid items.
- Take appropriate food and eating utensils.
- Take proper clothing appropriate for the given climate.
- Take a cellular phone if you would use it.
- Take binoculars and/or a camera if they would be useful and space allows.

This general list is NOT all inclusive. Be sure to investigate proper equipment needs for your specific adventure.

Mental Preparation

Mental preparation is critical to the success of an adventure. It begins with having positive expectations and a positive attitude about the adventure. To maintain a positive attitude as you prepare and plan for the adventure, imagine yourself successfully achieving your adventure goal. Keep that picture in your mind and play it over and over as if it were a videotape. This will help keep you motivated and help you "walk the walk and talk the talk" of your adventure. Keeping your mind focused on the ultimate goal and the timeline set forth, as well as seeing yourself in the role of adventurer, should keep you energized and inspired.

Sometimes during the final preparation stages of an adventure, your mind may get too wired, and you may experience difficulty in relaxing. Relaxation and stress reduction techniques will be essential for you before, during, and after the adventure! Some symptoms you may experience prior to the adventure could be restlessness or excessive sleeping, depression, feeling hungry all the time or never eating, crying for no reason, or feeling like your life is out of control. Part of this stress could be due to fear–perhaps fear of trying something new or fear of failing. Remember to keep focused on your goal and visualize yourself successfully completing the event. Positive expectations will help!

Another stress may come from the anticipation of the event itself. Try to keep focused on completing each item on your timeline and continue to do your homework on all aspects of the adventure.

During the actual adventure, you may experience stress in one of the following ways:

- Sweaty hands
- Cold hands and feet
- Warm face, cheeks, and ears
- Pressure headache
- Dry mouth
- Upset stomach or "butterflies" in your stomach

These are physical sensations related to stress. Different people will experience them to a greater or lesser degree, but they are perfectly normal reactions. Use these body changes as early warning signals to do something about the stress.

Here are some suggestions for stress reduction and relaxing:

- Engage in some *fun* physical activity.

- Eat healthy foods.

- Meditate by being physically still while maintaining an alert but neutral mental state.

- Listen to relaxing music.

- Concentrate on breathing with a slow and deliberate release of air.

- Turn to someone who will be an active listener and sounding board for you–a supportive adult, your favorite friend, or a counselor.

- Engage your sense of humor.

These techniques will help you get control, settle down, and recenter yourself. Your body needs a chance to rest and recover from the stress and strain of preparing for and engaging in an adventure.

Logical Precautions

During the processes involved with physical and mental preparation, it is also wise to consider logical precautions. You want your adventure to be as safe as possible, so there are necessary safeguards you must consider. Taking the necessary logical precautions also assists you in gaining the most from your adventure. Use the following checklist to help you head for a safe and secure adventure:

1. Have you done your research on all safety issues related to your adventure (library research, interviews with professionals in the field, and others who have been on a similar adventure, etc.)?

2. Have you participated in safety/training/preparation workshops available in your area?

3. Have you received medical clearance from your physician to participate in the adventure?

4. Do you have a clear understanding of your physical or other limitations?

5. Have you worked with a well-trained professional during the preparation process?

6. Do you have a well-trained and prepared partner to accompany you?

7. Have you checked all equipment and gear to be sure it is working properly?

Perseverance in Confronting Obstacles

As with any worthwhile pursuit, you may experience various obstacles as you proceed toward your goal. Here is where your real strength, character, wisdom, and endurance may be tested. From financial constraints to geographical limitations to lack of support from family and friends, you may be faced with some obstacles that could slow you down. Remember the saying "Where there's a will, there's a way." What does this mean to you? If you have a positive mental attitude and a strong sense of determination, you can accomplish most anything! The children's book *The Little Engine That Could* comes to mind when courage, a positive attitude, and determination are needed. Read it if you need a quick dose of an "I CAN" attitude. You must be ready to stay with your goal, be strong and persistent! Consider the following quote:

Press On

Nothing in the world can take the place of persistence. Talent will not; nothing is more common than unsuccessful men with talent. Genius will not; unrewarded genius is almost a proverb. Education will not; the world is full of educated derelicts. Persistence and determination alone are omnipotent.

–Calvin Coolidge

Think about what this quote means to you. Who is the most successful person you know? How has that person been persistent? You might want to interview her/him to determine what strategies she/he uses when faced with obstacles.

Finding ways to go around, over, or right through the barriers facing you may also call upon your creative thinking skills. It may help to go through the creative problem solving process as you approach obstacles. Figure it out, brainstorm a variety of solutions, try one or more solutions, and get around that obstacle!

Use the following set of questions to guide you through the creative problem solving process. Write out your responses to the questions. The process will take time, but the rewards and solutions will be worth it.

Problem Generation

1. What are some of the challenges or obstacles keeping you from reaching your adventure goal?
2. What are the most critical problems or challenges?

Problem Clarification

1. What are some illustrations of the problem or how does it show itself?

2. What are the things that cause the problem?

3. What are further challenges caused by the problem?

4. What are other characteristics or dimensions of the problem?

Problem Identification

State the underlying problem as clearly and precisely as possible using these beginning phrases:

• *In what ways might I solve the problem of...*

• *How might I solve the problem of...*

Idea Finding

Brainstorm solutions of all types. Come up with as many ideas as you can. Quantity breeds quality. It's O.K. to be wild and free with your ideas.

• *What could I do?*

• *What could be changed?*

Finding a Solution

Evaluate each idea according to your needs. Weigh each against the factors that will make the solution possible or impossible.

• *Is it legal?*

• *Is it ethical?*

• *How much will it cost?*

• *Will it be long lasting?*

129

• *How much time and effort will it take?*

• *What will I be risking?*

Implementation of the Solution

Choose the solution that seems best to you and put it into action.

• *Who will do what?*

• *How will it be done?*

• *What timeline will you follow?*

If you get stuck or find new problems, start over again from a fresh perspective.

In the book, *A Whack on the Side of the Head: How to Unlock Your Mind for Innovation*, Roger von Oech reminds us of the following story:

The Two Frogs

Once upon a time, two frogs fell in a bucket of cream. The first frog, seeing that there was no way to get any footing in the liquid, accepted his fate and drowned. The second frog didn't like that approach. He started thrashing around in the cream and doing whatever he could to stay afloat. After a while, all of his churning turned the cream into butter, and he was able to hop out.

Moral: *If you think you can find the second right answer, you are more likely to do so.*

Don't Give Up on Yourself or Your Adventure!

Like many of the girls and young women adventurers in this book, you may experience exhilaration, exhaustion, and depression after the adventure is complete. First, be sure to give yourself a pat on the back for accomplishing your goal. Second, remember to record your thoughts and feelings in your *Adventure Journal*.

Not only may these words serve as a reminder of the wonderful experience you completed, but they may be an inspiration for you and others in years to come. The journal could also help guide you as you prepare for your next adventure. Did you say *next* adventure? Certainly! After you have had the opportunity to enjoy your achievement and you've given your body, mind, and pocketbook plenty of time to rest...get busy planning the next adventure! There may be no better way to gain a new sense of confidence, self respect, and passion about life. Happy adventuring!

Section III

What Others Have Said and Accomplished

Some Quotes
to Think About

As you begin to think about adventures you would like to have, some words of others may prove to be inspirational. As you read the helpful quotes from girls and adults, record the ones that mean the most to you and those that you may wish to share with your friends. Are there people in your family, neighborhood, or community whom you could call, e-mail, or talk to about their adventures, and from whom you could acquire additional positive quotations? Why don't you get started now?

Quotes From Girls and Young Women

Girls and young women have great ideas about adventures. The following quotes were collected anonymously from elementary and secondary school female students to ensure their privacy.

What are your views concerning adventures? Perhaps you would like to write your own quotes and keep them in your personal *Adventure Journal!*

- ## Why is it important for young women to go on adventures?

   "To develop new experiences, new memories, and possibly new perspectives."

   "So they can experience life to the fullest."

   "When girls go on adventures they learn many new things, get a higher self-esteem, and find more courage that helps them stand tall."

   "It's important for young women to go on adventures because they teach you how to work together and be a leader."

   "We need to build our self-confidence so we can be an influence on generations to come that they can be whatever they want to be."

   "It builds character, courage, and strength."

   "It's important for young women to go on adventures because it helps them discover talents and virtues in themselves. Young women can build character and self-esteem by testing their limits with adventures."

   "To help them learn to go out on their own sometimes, and to develop themselves as individuals. To show that they can do anything as well as anyone else."

   "A long time ago women were told to stay indoors because adventures were men things. Now that we have the opportunity to explore things of our own interest, we should take the opportunity."

"Young women need to go on adventures to prepare themselves for the real world and gain knowledge."

- **What do adventures help us learn?**

  "They help us learn about places and how to be courageous and brave!"

  "In a way, they test your ability to believe in yourself. So adventures help you learn your limits."

  "What the world holds in store for us."

  "They help us learn that not only physical strength is needed but also mental strength. They kind of give you that "I can do anything I want" feeling. They teach us that there is always something new to explore."

  "They help us problem solve and they help us learn who we are and what we can do."

  "How far our fears reach and what to do to overcome them."

  "They help us learn our boundaries and our weaknesses, but they also contribute to our goal to be bolder and stronger. Many times adventures aid us in becoming wiser about surroundings and areas that we had previously not come in contact with."

  "Adventures help us learn diversity and teach us many lessons that can only be taught through experience. You meet many new people, cultures, and customs."

Here are some additional quotes from adults.

- **Quotes From Adults**

> *"Adventure is the vitaminizing element in histories both individual and social."*
> —William Bolitho

> *"It is good to have an end to journey towards; but it is the journey that matters, in the end."*
> —Ursula K. Le Guin

> *"But the adventure, the conquest of an unknown country, the struggle against the impossible, all have a fascination which draws me with an irresistible force."*
> —Sven Anders Hedin

> *"This shall be my parting word—know what you want to do—then do it. Make straight for your goal and go undefeated in spirit to the end."*
> —Ernestine Schumann-Heink

> *"The life of an adventurer is the practice of the art of the impossible."*
> —William Bolitho

> *"The discovery of the North Pole is one of those realities which could not be avoided. It is the wages which human perseverance pays itself when it thinks that something is taking too long. The world needed a discover of the North Pole, and in all areas of social activity, merit was less important here than opportunity."*
> —Karl Kraus

"I can honestly say that I was never affected by the question of the success of an undertaking. If I felt it was the right thing to do, I was for it regardless of the possible outcome."
                    –Golda Meir

"It is always the adventurers who accomplish great things."
                    –Montesquieu

"You can't be brave if you've only had wonderful things happen to you."
                    –Mary Tyler Moore

"I had a great desire to take off and go somewhere in flight, never having done it."
                    –Ruth Law Oliver

"Adventure is something you seek for pleasure, or even for profit, like a gold rush or invading a country;...but experience is what really happens to you in the long run; the truth that finally overtakes you."
                    –Katherine Anne Porter

"You must do the thing you think you cannot do."
                    –Eleanor Roosevelt

"You may be disappointed if you fail, but you are doomed if you don't try."
                    –Beverly Sills

"Let me listen to me and not to them."
                    –Gertrude Stein

"One of the things about equality is not just that you be treated equally to man, but you treat yourself equally to the way you treat a man."
    –Marlo Thomas

"The test of an adventure is that when you're in the middle of it, you say to yourself, "Oh, now I've got myself into an awful mess; I wish I were sitting quietly at home." And the sign that something's wrong with you is when you sit quietly at home wishing you were out having lots of adventure."
    –Thornton Wilder

Girl and Women Adventurers Across the Centuries

For centuries girls and women have been adventurers. They have climbed mountains, broken records in sports, and achieved outstanding goals in all areas of adventure. Historically, women, although barred from some activities, have been at the forefront with their spirit of adventuring, unique planning skills, high self-esteem and sense of self-worth and have led the way for others. As you review this timeline, add to it any information you have about girls and women. Where will you be on a future timeline?

Timeline of Great Adventurers

While the stories highlighted in this book primarily describe adventures with a physical dimension, those depicted in this timeline present a broader scope.

43BC   Hortensia, a Greek, was the first woman to lead a march for women's rights and protests against unfair taxes on women.

1766   Jeanne Baret (France) was the first woman to sail around the world; she made the journey disguised as a man.

1784   Comtesse de Montalembert (France) was the first woman to fly in a tethered balloon.

1784   Madame Thible (France) was the first woman to fly in an untethered balloon.

1805   Sacagawea (U.S.A.), a Shoshoni Indian, was the only woman among forty men; she was guide and interpreter for the Lewis and Clark Expedition in the Louisiana Territory.

1810   Hester Stanhope (Great Britain) began travels that would keep her abroad for the rest of her life and was among the earliest British subjects to travel among the desert peoples of Egypt and Syria. She was often accompanied by a doctor, Charles Meryon, who later published *Memoirs* (1845) and *Travels* (1846) which contain much of her writing.

1812   Ann Judson and Harriet Newell (U.S.A.) were the first two American women sent abroad as missionaries, serving with their husbands in India on the Isle of France (Mauritius) and in Burma (Myanmar).

1835   Henrietta Hall Shuck (U.S.A.) became the first American woman missionary in China.

1836   Eliza Hart Spalding and Narcissa Whitman (U.S.A.) became the first women of European ancestry to cross the Rocky Mountains.

142

1836   U.S. missionary Marcus Whitman took his wife, Narcissa, and Eliza Spalding to the Pacific Northwest. They were the first white women to cross the continent.

1837   Mary Lyon (U.S.A.) founded the first women's college, Mount Holyoke Seminary, in Massachusetts.

1838   Henriette d'Angeville (France) became the first woman to climb Mont Blanc in the French Alps, organizing her own expedition and completing the climb over three days; two other woman had previously been carried to the summit.

1838   Grace Darling (Great Britain), an English lighthouse keeper's daughter, rescued the survivors of the foundering ship *Forfarshire* with help from her father, William, and won plaudits for her heroism.

1849   Elizabeth Blackwell (British-American) was the first woman to receive a medical degree in the United States from Geneva College, N.Y. after being rejected by other colleges. Since she was not hired by any clinic, she started her own, and a Quaker group referred patients to her.

1850   Harriet Tubman (U.S.A.), an escaped slave, single-handedly led more than 300 others, including her parents, to safety on the Underground Railroad.

1859   Idawalley Zoradis Lewis (U.S.A.), Narragansett Bay lighthouse keeper, rescued four Newport boys after their small sailboat capsized. None could swim, and all would have drowned without her aid.

1861   Sojourner Truth (U.S.A.) challenged injustice by insisting that a street car driver allow her to ride when he refused to carry her because she was Black. She got others involved to support her.

1864   Clara Barton (U.S.A.) volunteered to help with feeding and nursing wounded soldiers during the Civil War. She later supervised the search for missing soldiers. She served as the first president of the American Red Cross.

1869   Myra Bradwell (U.S.A.) was the first American woman lawyer. She passed the Illinois bar but was barred from practicing because of her sex. She continued to advocate for legal reforms.

1875   Calamity Jane (Martha Jane Burk, U.S.A.) joined General George Crook's expedition against the Sioux Indians, but was forced to return when it was learned she was a woman.

1876   Lady Ann Blunt (Great Britain), an English explorer, traveled across the desert from Alelppo to Baghdad, skirting the Bedouin Tribes that inhabited the region.

1878   "Cockeyed Charlie" Parkhurst (U.S.A.), a California stagecoach driver, died of cancer at age 67 in a cabin near Watsonville. An autopsy later revealed that "Charlie" was a woman–Charlotte Darkey Parkhurst.

1879   Annie Oakley (Phoebe Anne Oakley Moses, U.S.A.) defeated Frank Butler in a shooting match; they later married and became touring partners with Buffalo Bill's Wild West Show, touring widely in North America and Europe. In 1889, she shot a cigarette from the mouth of Germany's Kaiser William II.

1881   Clara Barton (U.S.A.) was named the first president of the American Red Cross. She had been active during the Civil War in taking medical supplies to the front line and was given the position of Superintendent of Union Nurses.

1885   Sara Goode (U.S.A.) was the first African-American woman to earn a patent; the patent was for a folding bed similar to today's futon or sofa bed.

1887   Charlotte "Lottie" Dod (Great Britain) was the youngest woman (age 15) to win the women's singles tennis title at Wimbledon. She won this title four more years as well.

1890   Nellie Bly (Elizabeth Cochrane Seaman, U.S.A.) became world famous when she went around the world by boat, train, and horse in just slightly over seventy-two days.

1892   Mary Kingsley (Great Britain) began her travels in West Africa and returned to England with a collection of insects, reptiles, and fish (three would be named after her), which she donated to the British Museum. She published *Travels in West Africa* in 1897.

1893   Alexandra David-Neel (France) began her long series of journeys in Central Asia, which would occupy her life and be self-recorded in many books.

1894   Isabella Bird Bishop (Great Britain) published *Journeys in Persia and Kurdistan.* She also wrote *Hawaiian Archipelago, Unbeaten Tracks in Japan,* and *The Yangtze Valley and Beyond.*

1895   Octavie Coudreau (France) traveled with her husband, Henri Coudreau, to Para in northern Brazil. They co-authored six books about their journeys.

1895   Annie Peck (U.S.A.) won wide attention by climbing the Matterhorn dressed in a tunic and knickerbockers. She followed this with numerous other ascents, notably in the Alps and in Central and South America.

1896   Women (U.S.A.) played their first intercollegiate basketball game between the University of California at Berkeley and Stanford University; no males were allowed at the Berkeley game.

1898   Mary Ann Shadd Cary (U.S.A.), an educator and abolitionist, became the first Black woman to graduate from Howard University Law School in Washington, D.C., and the first Black woman to vote in a federal election.

1898   Dr. Anita Newcomb McGee (U.S.A.) was instrumental in creating the Army Nurse Corps (ANC), which provided trained military nurses to the armed forces during the Spanish-American War.

1901   Constance Applebee (U.S.A.) introduced field hockey to the United States, the first game being played at Harvard with ice hockey sticks.

1902   Harriet Hawes (U.S.A.), an archeologist, was the first female to direct a major field project with a crew of more than 100. She discovered and excavated a Minean settlement in Crete, and she was the first woman to report research to the Archeological Institute of America.

1903   Dorothea Douglass (Great Britain) won the first of what would be seven women's singles tennis titles at Wimbledon. She might have had more, but Wimbledon was not held for five years during World War I. She returned to the finals in 1919 and 1920.

1904   Annie Peck (U.S.A.) made the first ascent of Mt. Sorata in Bolivia.

1904   Annie Taylor (Great Britain) joined the Younghusband expedition in Lhasa as a nurse; she was the first woman to enter Tibet and traveled disguised as a pilgrim with a servant as her companion. She traveled 1300 miles before being discovered.

1907   Dorothy Tyler (U.S.A.) won a horse race in Joplin, Missouri, against experienced male riders, becoming America's first woman jockey.

1908   Annie Peck (U.S.A.) made the first ascent of the south peak of Huascaran in the Peruvian Andes. She climbed the Matterhorn in 1895, and continued to climb until she was 82 years old.

1909   The first all-woman auto race was run, a trip from New York City to Philadelphia and back.

1911   Harriett Quimby was the first American woman to earn a pilot's license, to make the first night flight, and the first female pilot to cross the English Channel.

1912   Fanny Durack, an Australian swimmer, won the women's 100-meter freestyle (the only women's swimming event) at the Stockholm Olympics, setting the first of her nine world records.

1912   Katherine Stinson was the first woman to be sworn in by the United States Post Office as a pioneer air mail carrier.

1913   Georgia Broadwick became the first American woman to parachute from an airplane.

1915   Mary Roberts Rinehart became the first American correspondent to report from the front line during World War I, and was the first to interview Queen Mary of Britain.

1918   Gertrude Ederle (U.S.A.) set her first world record in the 800-yard freestyle at age twelve and used the six-beat crawl introduced by the New York Women's Swimming Association. In 1926, she became the first woman to swim the English Channel from Cape Grix-Nez in France to Dover, England, and set a new record of 14 hours 39 minutes.

1919   Sophia Heath (U.S.A.), an American athletics admin-
        istrator and aviator, was the first woman commercial
        airplane pilot and founded the Women's Amateur
        Athletic Association (1922).

1922   Lilian Gatlin (U.S.A.) was the first woman to cross
        the continent by airplane.

1923   America's Amateur Athletic Union first admitted
        women. Acceptable sports included basketball,
        swimming, handball, gymnastics, and track and field.

1924   Alexandra David-Neel (France), disguising herself as
        a poor Tibetan, traveled in Tibet, reaching Lhasa.

1926   Frieda Carter (U.S.A.) invented miniature golf and
        was part owner of the Fairyland Inn resort. She
        patented her "Tom Thumb Golf" in 1929. By 1930
        there were 25,000 to 50,000 miniature golf courses.

1926   Phyllis Green, a British athlete, cleared the five-foot
        barrier in the high jump, becoming the first woman to
        do so.

1926   Helen Wills Moody (U.S.A.) began her domination
        of women's tennis, winning 31 titles (1926-1938),
        including a then-record eight women's singles titles
        at Wimbledon.

1928   Sonja Henje (Norway) won the first of her three
        Olympic gold medals for ice-skating. The previous
        year, she had won the first of her 10 world skating
        championships.

1928   Margaret Mead (U.S.A.), the first female anthropologist, traveled to Samoa to study the culture and wrote the book, *Coming of Age in Samoa.*

1928   Gertrude Caton-Thompson, a British archeologist, excavated ruins in Zimbabwe.

1929   Ellen Church (U.S.A.) became the first airline stewardess, having suggested the idea to Boeing Air Transport (later United Airlines). She recruited other stewardesses, originally all nurses like herself.

1930   Amy Johnson, a British aviatrix, arrived in Australia after making the first solo flight by a woman from London.

1931   Beryl Markham (Great Britain) became a commercial pilot, transporting mail and passengers throughout East Africa. Raised as one of the few Anglo children in Kenya, East Africa, she became a bush pilot leading aerial hunting expeditions. In 1936, she flew from London to Nova Scotia—the first person to have completed such an east to west solo flight. She wrote of these adventures in *West with the Night.*

1931   Jackie Mitchell (U.S.A.), 17, a minor league pitcher, signed a contract to pitch for the Memphis Lookouts in the Southern Association. She took the mound in April against the New York Yankees in an exhibition game at Chattanooga, Tennessee, and struck out Babe Ruth in four pitches and Lou Gehrig in three.

1931   "Babe" Didrikson Zaharias (U.S.A.) became the first internationally recognized woman athlete at the 1932 Los Angeles Olympic Games, where she won gold medals in the javelin throw and hurdles and tied for first in the high jump.

1931   Annie Peck, 82, (U.S.A.) made her final ascent of New Hampshire's Mt. Madison, and published *Flying over South America–20,000 Miles by Air.*

1932   Amelia Earhart (U.S.A.) landed in Northern Ireland after having made the first solo transatlantic flight by a woman. In 1937, she attempted to fly around the world but disappeared in the Pacific Ocean.

1932   Frances Perkins (U.S.A.) was named the first female to a cabinet position as Secretary of Labor.

1934   Conchita Cintron (U.S.A.) first publicly appeared on horseback in a bullfight ring at age 12 as a *rejoneadora.*

1934   Mary Hirsch became the first American woman licensed to train thoroughbred horses.

1935   Jean Gardner Batten (New Zealand) at age 25 flew a Gypsy Moth from England to New Zealand in a record 11 days.

1936   Krystyna Chojnowska-Liskiewicz (Poland) was the first yachtswoman to sail single-handedly around the world.

1937   Conchita Cintrón (U.S.A.) began fighting as a *torera* in Mexico at age 15. During her career she killed 400 bulls on foot as a *torera* and 800 on horseback.

1937   Doria Kopsky (U.S.A.) was the first woman to win the National Amateur Bicycle Association tournament.

1938   Valentina Grizodubova (Russia), pilot, gained world fame when she and two female companions broke the women's distance record, flying 4,000 miles in one direction from Moscow to the Far East.

1941   Louise Brough and Margaret Osborne (U.S.A.) won the first of nine successive U.S. doubles tennis titles.

1942   Margaret Bourke-White (U.S.A.) was the first woman accredited as a war correspondent and crossed the German border with the troops of General Patton.

1943   Judy Johnson (U.S.A.) was the first woman steeple-chase rider at a major U.S. track.

1946   Patty Berg, a golfer, defeated Betty Jameson in the final round of the first U.S. Women's Open. She was named Female Athlete of the Year in 1938, 1943, and 1955.

1946   Catherine Booth (Great Britain) led the Salvation Army's war relief efforts for children after World War II, as she had done after World War I.

1946   Edith Houghton (U.S.A.) became a scout for the Philadelphia Phillies, the first woman scout for a major league baseball team.

1947   Juliette Gordon Lowe founded Girl Scouts of the U.S.A.

1948   Clara Barton founded the American Red Cross.

1948   Fanny Blankers-Koen, a Dutch track and field athlete, won four gold medals at the London Olympics.

1948   Mother Teresa (Agnes Gronxha Bojaxhiu, Macedonia), a Roman Catholic Missionary, left her convent to tend to the sick, starving, and homeless in Calcutta, India. She took extremely ill people from the streets into a home to die peacefully. In 1979, she received the Nobel Peace Prize.

1948   "Babe" Didrikson Zaharias (U.S.A.) and a group of women golfers founded the Ladies Professional Golf Association. She was later named by the Associated Press as "the greatest female athlete of the first half of the twentieth century."

1949   Marian Laddewig, a U.S. bowler, won the first national All-Star games open to women.

1950   Florence Chadwick (U.S.A.) swam the English Channel and beat the record set by Gertrude Ederle in 1926.

1950   Maureen Connolly (U.S.A.) won the U.S. singles tennis title at age 16.

1950   Althea Gibson (U.S.A.) became the first African-American tennis player to play at Wimbledon. She reached the quarterfinals.

1951   Florence Chadwick (U.S.A.) was the first woman to swim from England to France and from Los Angeles to Catalina Island. In 1953, she made a "grand slam" of four channel swims in five weeks, each one a record setter: England to France across the English Channel, across the Strait of Gibraltar, across the Bosporus and back, and across the Dardanelles.

1953   Jeanette Burr (Switzerland) won the Swiss National Ski Championship at Grindelwald.

1953   Maureen Connolly (U.S.A.) became the first woman to win a Grand Slam in tennis, winning at Wimbledon and at the American, French, and Australian opens.

1954   Tenley Albright (U.S.A.) completed a six year comeback from poliomyelitis by winning the world figure-skating championship in Davos, Switzerland, at age 17.

1954   Jacqueline Cochran (U.S.A.), piloting a Sabre jet, became the first woman to break the sound barrier.

1955   Louise Boyd, an American explorer of the Arctic Ocean, was the first woman to fly over the North Pole. She was 68 years old.

1955   Rosa Parks (U.S.A.) refused to give up her seat to a white passenger on a bus in Montgomery, Alabama. She was arrested and fined fourteen dollars.

1956   Iolanda Balas (Romania) set a world record in the high jump; she would extend that record 13 more times (1956-1961).

1956   Autherine Juanita Lucy (U.S.A.) was the first Black student admitted to the University of Alabama at Tuscaloosa. She attended classes, was suspended "for her own safety." Later, the U.S. District Court ruled that the university must readmit her.

1957   Patricia McCormick entered the arena at Ciudad Juarez, Mexico, as the first U.S. woman bullfighter.

1957   Althea Gibson (U.S.A.) won in women's singles at Wimbledon. She was the first African American to be invited to play there.

1958   Catherine Machado (U.S.A.) became the first U.S. Hispanic to win the World Professional Figure Skating Championship.

1959   Mary Leakey, a British paleoanthropologist, found the 1,750,000 year old skull of Zinjanthropers in Africa. In 1975, she found the 3,7500,000 year old jaws and teeth of a Homo species and the fossilized footprints of a bipedal hominid in 1979.

1959   Wilma Rudolph (U.S.A.) won Olympic gold medals in the 100 meters, the 200 meters, and the relay.

1960   Jane Goodall (Great Britain) arrived in Tanzania for the longest study of wild chimpanzees in their natural habitat. In 1977, she founded The Jane Goodall Institute to continue support for chimpanzee research.

1961   Charlayne Hunter-Gault (U.S.A.) was one of two African American students to desegregate the University of Georgia in Atlanta.

1961   Billie Jean King (U.S.A.) won a doubles title at Wimbledon. It was the first of what would be 20 Wimbledon titles.

1961   Wilma Rudolph (U.S.A.) set a new women's record at Stuttgart, running the 100-meter dash in 11.2 seconds.

1962   Rachel Carson (U.S.A.) published her book, *Silent Spring,* which described the effects of pesticides and helped awareness of the need for environmental legislation.

1964   Jacqueline Cochran (U.S.A.) logged a speed of 1,429 miles per hour–the fastest ever flown by a woman.

1964   Geraldine Mock (U.S.A.) completed a solo round-the-world flight becoming the first woman to accomplish the feat.

1966   Rosemary Casals (U.S.A.) won the Wimbledon women's doubles tennis championship with Billie Jean King and became the first U.S. Hispanic woman to become a top ranked tennis professional.

1967   The Boston Marathon included a runner who had registered under the name K. Switzer and turned out to be Katherine Switzer. Race officials tried to remove her number, creating an uproar. The American Athletic Union issued a ruling that forbade women to compete in the same events with men on pain of losing their rights to compete anywhere. Switzer fought the ruling, and in 1972, the marathon was opened to women.

1968   Vera Caslavska (Czechoslovakia) won four gold and two silver medals in gymnastics at the Mexico Olympics, one gold for her "Mexican-hat dance" floor routine. Her wins were especially notable because she had to train in hiding, as Soviet troops were suppressing the Czech independence movement.

1968   Birute Galdikas, a Canadian anthropologist, began living in the rainforests in Borneo. She established orangutan support groups all over the world.

1968   Kathy Kusner became the first licensed woman jockey in U.S. racing.

1968   The National Women's Hall of Fame was founded at Seneca Falls, New York, on the site of the 1848 women's right convention.

1969   Penny Ann Early (U.S.A.), the first woman to play professional basketball, played a single game with the Kentucky Colonels team of the American Basketball Association.

1969   Sharon Sites Adams (U.S.A.) sailed solo across the Pacific, the first woman to do so.

1969   Shirley Chisolm (U.S.A.) was the first African-American woman elected to Congress.

1970   The first all-woman climb to the Denali summit at Mt. McKinley in Alaska was made by a team including Arlene Blum (U.S.A.). She later led a team that climbed Annapurna.

1970   Diane Crump became the first woman jockey to ride in the Kentucky Derby.

1971   Bella Abzug (U.S.A.) was the first Jewish woman elected to Congress.

1972   Athletic scholarships for American women were first offered by the University of Chicago, where organized American women's collegiate athletics had effectively started in 1898.

1972   Olga Korbut (Russia) won three gold medals in gymnastics at the Munich Olympics, becoming the first person to do a backward somersault on the uneven parallel bars in competition and the first woman to do a backflip on the balance beam.

1972   Sally J. Priesand (U.S.A.) was ordained the first American rabbi in Trenton Falls, N.J.

1973   Lynne Cox (U.S.A.) swam the English Channel in 9 hours, 36 minutes—a new world record for both women and men.

1973   The Women's Tennis Association was founded by a group that included Billie Jean King, seeking to have women's pay, perks, and prestige equal that accorded to men. That same year King played in a highly publicized "battle of the sexes" match, beating male challenger Bobby Riggs (1939 Wimbledon champion).

1973   Women bullfighters were for the first time able to fight as *toreras* on foot in the bullfight ring in Spain, after Spanish bullfighter Angelita (Angela) Hernandez won her fight to do so; from 1908, women *toreras* had been barred, though some had defied the ban.

1974   Phyllis Ackerman (U.S.A.) was the first woman to provide sports commentary for a professional basketball team, the Indiana Pacers.

1974   Chris Evert (U.S.A.) won the first of her three women's singles tennis tournaments at Wimbledon.

1974   Martina Navratilova (Czechoslovakia) defected to the U.S.A. and went on to become the top-ranked woman tennis player in the world.

1975   Tabei Junko (Japan) was the first woman to reach the top of Mt. Everest.

1976   Krystyna Chojnowska-Liskiewicz (Poland) was the first woman to sail solo around the world in her yacht *Mazurek*.

1976   Mary Leakey (Great Britain) found trails of fossilized footprints in Africa that proved human ancestors walked upright 3.6 million years ago.

1976   Kitty O'Neil (U.S.A.) was the first woman member of Hollywood's Stunts Unlimited.

1977   Clare Francis (Great Britain) was the first woman to captain a boat in the Whitbread Round the World Event (1977-1978), coming in fifth with her crew of 11.

1977   Janet Guthrie (U.S.A.) became the first woman to qualify and race in the Indianapolis 500. Driving with a broken wrist, she came in eighth.

1977   Shirley Muldowney (U.S.A.) became the first woman to win the National Hot Rod Association's Winston World Championship of drag racing; she would later win twice more.

1978   Arlene Blum (U.S.A.) organized and led the American Women's Himalayan Expedition to Annapurna. Two women, Krene Miller and Vera Komarkova, with two sherpas, reached the top.

1978   Brigadier General Mary Clarke (U.S.A.) became the army's first woman two-star major general.

1978   Penny Dean (U.S.A.) set a new English Channel speed record swimming the 20-mile distance from England to France in 7 hours, 42 minutes.

1978   Golfer Nancy Lopez (U.S.A.) won her first championships as a professional, the Bent Tree Classic, later winning a record five consecutive tournaments and the European Ladies tournament.

1979   Silvia Ortiz (U.S.A.) became the first U.S. Hispanic to compete on a U.S. team at the Pan American games, in softball.

1980   Crystal Fields (U.S.A.), age 11, won the Pitch, Hit, and Run Championship, the first girl to win the national baseball playoff open to both sexes.

1980   Adriana C. Ocampo (U.S.A.) has worked since high school for the National American Space agency (NASA); now a planetary geologist, she is involved in missions to Mars.

1981   Tonia Schlegel (U.S.A.), 13, of Hamilton, Ohio, won the annual All-American Soap-Box Derby becoming the first girl to capture the event.

1983   Sally Ride (U.S.A.) was the first American woman to fly in space. She was mission specialist aboard the Space Shuttle Challenger.

1984   Wangari Maathai (Africa) was the first Kenyan woman to obtain a doctorate. After studying biology in the United States, she returned to Africa to grow seedlings and eventually supply Kenya with a million trees for a green belt.

1984   Svetlana Savitskaya (Russia), on July 25, 1984, became the first woman to walk in space.

1984   Dr. Kathryn Sullivan (U.S.A.) on October 11, 1984, became the first U.S. woman to perform an extravehicular activity in space. She was one of the seven member Challenger crew.

1985   Sylvia Earle (U.S.A.) set a record for solo diving in a submersible–3,280 feet.

1985   Wilma Mankiller (U.S.A.) became Principal Chief of the Cherokee Nation after she brought about many improvements in health, education, and government for her people.

1985   Nancy Lopez (U.S.A.) won the Ladies Professional Golf Association title and set a winning record with over $416,000.

1985   Libby Riddles (U.S.A.) became the first woman to win Alaska's Iditarod Trail Sled Dog Race.

1985   Lynette Woodard (U.S.A.) became the first woman to play regularly on the previously all-male Harlem Globetrotters basketball team (1985-1987).

1986   Ann Bancroft (U.S.A.) was the first and only woman to reach the North Pole by dogsled.

1987   Steffi Graf (Germany) emerged as the world's leading woman tennis player, with 66 consecutive victories, and continued to dominate women's tennis for long periods through the early 1990s.

1987   Mae Jemison (U.S.A.) became the first African American in NASA's training program for astronauts. She and the others were selected from 2000 applicants. In 1992, she flew in the shuttle Endeavor for eight days, 127 rotations around the earth. She also worked in West Africa in the Peace Corps and earned an MD degree. She later resigned from NASA and founded the Jemison Group for research and development of technological advances.

1987   Gayle Sierens (U.S.A.) was the first woman to do play-by-play coverage of a major league football game.

1988   Florence Griffith Joyner (U.S.A.) broke the world record for the hundred meter dash by three-tenths of a second. She was the fastest woman in the world.

1989   Victoria Brucker (U.S.A.) was the first girl to reach the Little League World Series.

1989   Julie Croteau (U.S.A.) became the first woman to play on an American men's college varsity baseball team at St. Mary's College, Maryland; while in high school in Prince William County, Virginia, she had played on the junior varsity team, but lost a lawsuit to join the varsity squad (1988).

1990   Susan Butcher (U.S.A.) set a new course record in winning her fourth Anchorage-Nome Iditarod Trail Sled Dog Race. She won the race in 1986, 1987, 1988, and 1990.

1990   Brigadier General Marcelite Harris (U.S.A.) was the first African-American woman general in the Air Force.

1991   The first women's World Cup soccer final was held at Guangzhou (Canton). The U.S. team beat Norway two games to one.

1992   Jackie Joyner-Kersee (U.S.A.) won an unprecedented second Olympic gold medal in the heptathlon.

1993   Eugenie Clark (U.S.A.) won the National Geographic Society Franklin Burr Award, one of over 43 awards for her studies and films on shark behaviors.

1993   Julie Krone (U.S.A.) won the Belmont Stakes, becoming the first woman jockey to win one of America's "Triple Crown" races.

1993   Ellen Ochoa (U.S.A.) became the first Hispanic woman to be part of a space mission crew and flew in the shuttle Discovery. Also a respected engineer, she holds three patents in optical processing.

1993   Sheryl Swoopes (U.S.A.) scored a game record 47 points in the NCAA National Championships.

1995   Eileen Collins (U.S.A.) became the first woman to be selected to be a space shuttle pilot. In July 1999, she launched the Columbia into space. She took with her a scarf once worn by fellow pioneer Amelia Earhart.

1996   Rebecca Lobo (U.S.A.) became the first Hispanic woman basketball player to be named All American center.

1996   Shannon Lucid (U.S.A.), astronaut, set the record for the longest space flight by an American.

1996   Angela Moscarelli (U.S.A.) at the age of fourteen won the Junior World Target Championships.

1997   Madeleine Albright was appointed the first female Secretary of State of the U.S.

1997   Yvonne Trevino (U.S.A.) won the World Bantamweight Championship of the Women's International Boxing Federation.

1999   Doris Haddock (U.S.A.), known as Granny D., at age 89 has been walking across the U.S. to raise public awareness about campaign finance reform. She has walked ten miles a day six days a week hoping to make it from California to Washington D.C.

1999   Nancy Marc (U.S.A.) was the first woman to graduate from the Citadel, a previously all male military academy.

1999   Chih-Yuan Ho and Melissa Kay Graham (U.S.A.) graduated from Virginia Military Institute as the first females in the one hundred and sixty year history of the school.

1999   The U.S. Women's National Soccer Team won the Women's World Cup.

1999   Tori Murden (U.S.A.) became the first woman to row solo across the Atlantic Ocean, finishing the trip December 3rd after 81 days.

2000   Peggy Bouchet (France), at age 26, became the first French woman to row across the Atlantic alone, arriving at Martinique after 48 days at sea.

Adventure Books

You will learn a lot about adventures and challenges by reading books. Just as you have learned about adventures from the stories from the girls and young women is this book, you will enjoy other writings on the topic. Traveling and exploring are the focus of the selected books which follow. However, there are many more volumes which can be found in libraries and bookstores in your local community.

How to Books

American Red Cross. (1992). *Swimming and diving*. St. Louis, MO: Mosby Year Book.

Armentrout, D. (1997). *Sports challenge*. Vero Beach, FL: Rourke Publishing Group.

Armentrout, D. (1998). *Outdoor adventures*. Vero Beach, FL: Rourke Publishing Group.

Armentrout, D., & Armentrout, P. (1998). *Compete like a champion-hockey*. Vero Beach, FL: Rourke Publishing Group.

Arnosky, J. (1991). *Fish in a flash! A personal guide to spinfishing*. New York, NY: Bradbury Press.

Bavier, B. (1983). *Sailing to win*. New York, NY: Dodd, Mead & Company.

Blount, S., & Taylor, H. (1984). *The joy of snorkeling*. New York, NY: Collier Books.

Bonney, B. (1998). *Play it like a pro-softball*. Vero Beach, FL: Rourke Publishing Group.

Boulais, S. (1992). *Learning how: BMX biking*. Marco, FL: Bancroft-Sage Publishing.

Brenner, J. R. (1990). *Make the team: Basketball a slammin' jammin' guide to super hoops!* Boston, MA: A Sports Illustrated For Kids Book.

Brenner, J. R. (1990). *Make the team: Soccer a heads-up to super soccer!* Boston, MA: A Sports Illustrated For Kids Book.

Brown, J. (1995). *Tennis: Steps to success*. Champaign, IL: Human Kinetics.

Bryant, J. (1997). *Game set match: A tennis guide*. Englewood, CO: Morton Publishing Company.

Carmichael, C., & Burke, E. (1994). *Fitness cycling: Fitness spectrum series*. Champaign, IL: Human Kinetics.

Carson, C., Jr. (1991). *Make the team: Swimming/diving.* Boston, MA: A Sports Illustrated For Kids Book.

Combs, C. (1988). *Soaring: Where hawks and eagles fly.* New York, NY: Henry Holt and Company.

Cooper, M. (1988). *Racing sled dogs: An original North American sport.* New York, NY: Ticknor & Fields.

Craig, S., & Johnson, K. (1985). *The softball handbook.* West Point, NY: Leisure Press.

David, A., & Moran, T. (1983). *River thrill sports.* Minneapolis, MN: Lerner Publications Company.

Edwards, S., & McKenzie, M. (1995). *Snowshoeing: Outdoor pursuits series.* Champaign, IL: Human Kinetics.

Ford, K. (1995). *White water and sea kayaking.* Champaign, IL: Human Kinetics.

Gensemer, R. (1994). *Tennis for experienced players.* Englewood, CO: Morton Publishing Company.

Griffiths, T. (1985). *Sport SCUBA diving in depth: An introduction to basic scuba instruction and beyond.* Princeton, NJ: Princeton Book Company.

Grosshandler, J. (1991). *Winning ways in soccer.* New York, NY: Cobblehill Books.

Hackwell, J. (1988). *Diving to the past: Recovering ancient wrecks.* New York, NY: Charles Scribner's Sons.

169

Haycock, K. (1991). *Olympic sports: Gymnastics.* New York, NY: Crestwood House.

Haycock, K. (1991). *Olympic sports: Skiing.* New York, NY: Crestwood House.

Jackman, J. (1995). *The young gymnast.* New York, NY: DK Publishing Co.

Jacobson, C. (1997). *The basic essentials of canoeing.* Merrillville, IN: ICS Books, Inc.

Jacobson, C. (1988). *The basic essentials of camping.* Merrillville, IN: ICS Books, Inc.

Johnson, N. (1991). *Fire and silk: Flying in a hot air balloon.* Boston, MA: Joy Street Books.

Joyner, S. (1995). *In-line roller hockey: The official guide and resource book.* Chicago, IL: Contemporary Books.

Kalman, B. (1995). *Crabapples: A canoe trip.* New York, NY: Crabtree Publishing Company.

Kalman, B., & Everts, T. (1997). *Gymnastics.* New York, NY: Crabtree Publishing Company.

Kelly, Z. (1998). *Compete like a champion-volleyball.* Vero Beach, FL: Rourke Publishing Group.

King, R. (1991). *Rad boards.* Boston, MA: A Sports Illustrated For Kids Book.

Kirksmith, T. (1991). *Ride western style: A guide for young riders*. New York, NY: Howell Book House.

Kozar, A., & Catignani, E. (1997). *Beginning racquetball.* Knoxville, TN: Hunter Textbooks.

Leder, J. M. (1991). *Learning how: Skateboarding.* Marco, FL: Bancroft-Sage Publishing.

Leder, J. M. (1992). *Learning how: Gymnastics.* Marco, FL Bancroft-Sage Publishing.

Leder, J. M. (1992). *Learning how: Karate.* Marco, FL: Bancroft-Sage Publishing.

LeMond's, G. (1987). *Complete book of bicycling.* New York, NY: The Puntnam Publishing Group.

Lloyd, B. (1997). *Play it like a pro-football.* Vero Beach, FL: Rourke Publishing Group.

Lloyd, B. (1998). *Play it like a pro-martial arts.* Vero Beach, FL: Rourke Publishing Group.

McMartin, B. (1993). *Adventure in hiking: An introduction to Adirondack hiking.* North Country.

Merrison, T. (1991). *Olympic sports: Field athletics.* New York, NY: Crestwood House.

Messner, Y. (1992). *Swimming everyone: Second edition.* Winston-Salem, NC: Hunter Textbooks Inc.

171

Mills, B. (1997). *Volleyball: Keys to success a beginning skills guide.* Dubuque, IA: Eddie Bowers Publishing, Inc.

Mitchel, D. (1992). *The young martial artist.* Woodstock, NY: The Overlook Press.

National Association of Underwater Instructors Staff (1994). *Adventures in scuba diving: A text for the beginning diver.* St. Louis, MO: Mosby Year Book.

Nicoson, M. (1993). *The basic essentials of bicycle touring.* Merrillville, IN: ICS Books, Inc.

Norton, C., & Bryant, J. (1986). *Beginning racquetball.* Englewood, CO: Morton Publishing Company.

O'Meara, D., & Murray, T. (1997). *The basic elements of sports series: Tennis unlimited.* Merrillville, IN: ICS Books, Inc.

Park, Y. H., & Leibowitz, J. (1993). *Taekwondo for children.* East Meadow, NY: Park Publications Ltd.

Potter, D., & Brockmeyer, G. (1989). *Teaching softball: Steps to success.* Champaign, IL: Leisure Press.

Reach, J., & Schwartz, B. (1992). *Softball everybody: Second edition.* Winston-Salem, N.C.: Hunter Textbooks Inc.

Reichenfeld, R., & Bruechert, A. (1995). *Snowboarding.* Champaign, IL: Human Kinetics.

Renfrew, T. (1997). *Orienteering.* Champaign, IL: Human Kinetics.

Rodenas, P. (1991). *The Random House book of horses and horsemanship.* New York, NY: Random House Inc.

Rouse, J. (1997). *The young swimmer.* New York, NY: DK Publishing Book.

Sandelson, R. (1991). *Olympic sports: Ball sports.* New York, NY: Crestwood House.

Sandelson, R. (1991). *Olympic sports: Combat sports.* New York, NY: Crestwood House.

Sandelson, R. (1991). *Olympic sports: Ice sports.* New York, NY: Crestwood House.

Sandelson, R. (1991). *Olympic sports: Track athletics.* New York, NY: Crestwood House.

Seaborg, E., & Dudley, E. (1994). *Hiking and backpacking.* Champaign, IL: Human Kinetics.

Stephenson, S. (1991). *Auto-cross racing.* New York, NY: Crestwood House.

Stephenson, S. (1991). *Circle track racing.* New York, NY: Crestwood House.

Stephenson, S. (1991). *Rally racing.* New York, NY: Crestwood House.

Stephenson, S. (1991). *Winston Cup racing.* New York, NY: Crestwood House.

Stine, M. (1990). *Wheels: The kids' bike book.* Boston, MA: A Sports Illustrated For Kids Book.

Watts, P. (1996). *Rock climbing.* Champaign, IL: Human Kinetics.

Whitlock, S. (1991). *Make the team gymnastics for girls.* Boston, MA: A Sports Illustrated For Kids Book.

Winner, K. (1995). *Wind surfing: Outdoor pursuits series.* Champaign, IL: Human Kinetics.

Urban, J. (1981). *White water handbook.* Boston, MA: Appalachian Mountain Club.

Books For Youth

Atkinson, L. (1985). *In kindling flame: The story of Hannah Senesh 1921-1944*. New York, NY: Lothrop.

Ayer, E. (1992). *Margaret Bourke-White: Photographing the world*. New York: Dillon Press.

Bennett, W. E. (1973). *Women who dared to be different*. Champaign, IL: Garrard.

Bennett, W. E. (1975). *Four women of courage*. Champaign, IL: Garrard.

Berleth, R. (1994). *Mary Patten's voyage*. New York, NY: Albert Whitman.

Blacknall, C. (1984). *Sally Ride: American's first woman in space*. Minneapolis, MN: Dillon Press, Inc.

Blos, J. W. (1996). *Nellie Bly's monkey: His remarkable story in his own words*. New York, NY: Morrow.

Briggs, C. S. (1991). *At the controls: Women in aviation*. Minneapolis, MN: Lerner Publishing Group.

Browne, R. B. (1990). *Contemporary heroes and heroines.* Detroit, MI: Gale Research Inc.

Brown, D. (1993). *Ruth Law thrills a nation.* New York, NY: Ticknor & Fields.

Brown, D. P. (1985). *Sybil rides for independence.* New York, NY: Albert Whitman.

Bunfield, S. (Ed.) (1987). *Joan of Arc: French patriot.* Broomall, PA: Chelsea House Publishers.

Burns, B. (1994). *Harriet Tubman.* Broomall, PA: Chelsea House Publishers.

Camp, C. A. (1997). *Sally Ride: First American woman in space.* Springfield, NJ: Enslow Publishing, Inc.

Chadwick, R. (1987). *Amelia Earhart: Aviation pioneer.* Minneapolis, MN: Lerner Publishing Group.

Christopher, T. (1993). *Joan of Arc: Soldier saint.* Broomall, PA: Chelsea House Publishers.

Clyne, P. (1976). *Patriots in petticoats.* New York, NY: Dodd, Mead.

Cohen, J. H. (1997). *Superstars of women's gymnastics.* Broomall, PA: Chelsea House Publishers.

Conley, A. (1991). *Window on the deep: The adventures of underwater explorer Sylvia Earle.* New York: Franklin Watts.

Cordell, J., & Cordell, C. (1997). *Adventurous tales of the Allspot family.* Lexington, MA: Banquet Books.

Cousteau Society Staff (1992). *An adventure in New Zealand.* Old Tappan, NJ: S&S Childrens.

Crump, D. J. (1989). *Adventures in your national parks.* Washington, DC: National Geographic.

Dawson, S. (1960). *A confederate girl's diary.* Bloomington, IN: Indiana University Press.

Dewey, J. O. (1994). *Wildlife rescue: The work of Dr. Kathleen Ramsay.* Honesdale, PA: Boyds Mills.

Donohue, S. (1994). *Kristi Yamaguchi.* Minneapolis, MN: Lerner Publishing Group.

Edelson, P. (1998). *Nancy Kerrigan.* Broomall, PA: Chelsea House Publishers.

Flynn, J. (1998). *Annie Oakley: Legendary sharpshooter.* Springfield, NJ: Enslow Publishers, Inc.

Fromer, J. (1992). *Jane Goodall: Living with the chimps.* Frederick, MD: Twenty-First Century Books.

Fuchs, C. (1993). *Jackie Joyner-Kersee.* Vero Beach, FL: Rourke Publishing Group.

Fuchs, C. (1993). *Jane Goodall.* Vero Beach, FL: Rourke Publishing Group.

Gaines, A. G. (1999). *Female firsts in their fields: Women in sports and athletics.* Broomall, PA: Chelsea House Publishers.

Gallardo, E. (1993). *Among the orangutans: The Birute' Galdikas story.* Moravia, NY: Chronicle.

Greene, C. (1991). *Elizabeth Blackwell: First woman doctor.* Minneapolis, MN: Children's Press.

Goldstein, M. J., & Larson, J. (1994). *Jackie Joyner-Kersee: Superwoman.* Minneapolis, MN: Lerner Publishing Group.

Goodall, J. (1996). *My life with the chimpanzees.* New York, NY: Pocket.

Griffin, J. B. (1977). *Phoebe the spy.* New York, NY: Scholastic.

Hamilton, L., & Horner, M. S. (1987). *Clara Barton-American Red Cross founder.* Broomall, PA: Chelsea House Publishers.

Harrington, D. J. (1995). *Top 10 women tennis players.* Springfield, NJ: Enslow Publishers, Inc.

Harrington, G. (1995). *Jackie Joyner-Kersee.* Broomall, PA: Chelsea House Publishers.

Harris, L. (1992). *Biography today: Profiles of people of interest to young readers.* Detroit, MI: Omniographics, Inc.

Harvey, B. C. (1999). *Jane Adams: Nobel prize winner and founder of Hull House.* Springfield, NJ: Enslow Publishers, Inc.

Higers, L. (1990). *Steffi Graf.* New York, NY: Little, Brown & Company.

Hooks, W. H. (1995). *The girl who could fly.* Old Tappan, NJ: Macmillan.

Ianrone, C. (1995). *Pocahontas: Powhatan princess.* Broomall, PA: Chelsea House Publishers.

Jeffrey, L. S. (1998). *Christa McAuliffe: A space biography.* Springfield, NJ: Enslow Publishers, Inc.

Katz, W. L. (1995). *Black women of the old west.* Old Tappan, NJ: Atheneum.

Kelly, E. B. (1998). *Katarina Witt.* Broomall, PA: Chelsea House Publishers.

Kelly, J. (1997). *Superstars of women's basketball.* Broomall, PA: Chelsea House Publishers.

Kendall, M. E. (1997). *Susan B. Anthony: Voice for women's voting rights.* Springfield, NJ: Enslow Publishers, Inc.

King, C. (1993). *Adventure stories.* New York, NY: Kingfisher Books.

King, C., & Irvin, H. (1993). *Rosa Parks: Civil rights leader.* Broomall, PA: Chelsea House Publishers.

Knapp, R. (1995). *Sports great Steffi Graf.* Springfield, NJ: Enslow Publishers, Inc.

Knudson, R.R. (1985). *Babe Didrikson: Athlete of the century.* New York, NY: Puffin.

Kramer, B. (1998). *Sally Ride: A space biography.* Springfield, NJ: Enslow Publishers, Inc.

Kramer, S. A. (1993). *Adventure in Alaska.* New York, NY: Random House.

Krone, J., & Richardson, N. A. (1995). *Riding for my life.* New York, NY: Little, Brown, & Company.

Krull, K. (1996). *Wilma unlimited: How Wilma Rudolph became the world's fastest woman.* San Diego, CA: Harcourt.

Lauber, P. (1988). *Lost star: The story of Amelia Earhart.* New York, NY: Scholastic.

Lee, H. (1984). *Heroes, villains, and ghosts: Folklore of old California.* Santa Barbara, CA: Capra Press.

Levin, P. (1993). *Susan B. Anthony: Fighter for women's rights.* Broomall, PA: Chelsea House Publishers.

Macy, S. (1996). *Winning ways: A photo history of American women in sports.* Cambridge, MA: Holt.

Meachum, V. (1997). *Jane Goodall: Protector of chimpanzees.* Springfield, NJ: Enslow Publisher, Inc.

McGovern, A. (1978). *Shark lady: True adventures of Eugenie Clark.* New York, NY: Scholastic.

McGovern, A. (1989). *Down under, down under: Diving adventures on the Great Barrier Reef.* New York, NY: Macmillan.

McKissack, P. and McKissack, F. (1991). *Ida B. Wells-Barnett.* Springfield, NJ: Enslow Publishers, Inc.

McMane, F., & Wolf, C. (1995). *Winning women: Eight great athletes and their unbeatable stories.* New York, NY: Bantam/Sports Illustrated for Kids.

Miller, B. M. (1995). *Buffalo gals: Women of the old west.* Minneapolis, MN: Lerner Publishing Group.

Miller, R. H. (1995). *The story of "Stagecoach" Mary Fields.* Parippany, NJ: Silver Press.

Molzahn, A. B. (1998). *Top 10 American women sprinters.* Springfield, NJ: Enslow Publishers, Inc.

Morrissette, M. (1991). *Jennifer Capriati.* New York, NY: Little, Brown, & Company.

Patterson, F. (1987). *Koko's story.* New York, NY: Scholastic.

Peavy, L., & Smith, U. (1985). *Dreams into deeds: Nine women who dared.* New York, NY: Charles Scribner's Sons.

Pond, M. M. (1991). *Mother Teresa: A life of charity.* Broomall, PA: Chelsea House Publishers.

Poynter, M. (1998). *Top 10 American women's figure skaters.* Springfield, NJ: Enslow Publishers, Inc.

Pringle, L. (1993). *Jackal woman: Exploring the world of jackals.* Old Tappan, NJ: Scribner.

Quackenbush, R. (1987). *Who's that girl with the gun: A story of Annie Oakley.* New York, NY: Prentice-Hall.

Quackenbush, R. (1990). *Clear the cow pasture, I'm coming in for a landing!: A story of Amelia Earhart.* New York, NY: Simon and Schuster.

Quackenbush, R. (1992). *Stop the presses, Nellie's got a scoop!* New York: Simon and Schuster.

Rappaport, D. (1991). *Living dangerously: American women who risked their lives for adventure.* New York, NY: Harper.

Reit, S. (1988). *Behind enemy lines.* San Diego, CA: Harcourt Brace Jovanovich.

Rice, T. (1998). *The life and times of Mother Teresa.* Broomall, PA: Chelsea House Publishers.

Ride, S. (1986). *To space and back.* New York, NY: Lothrop.

Rivera, G. (1976). *A special kind of courage: Profiles of young Americans.* New York, NY: Simon and Schuster.

Ross, N. W. (1960). *Heroines of the early west.* New York, NY: Random House.

Sakurai, G. (1995). *Mae Jemison: Space scientist.* Minneapolis, MN: Children's Press.

Sanford, W. R., & Green, C. R. (1996). *Calamity Jane: Frontier original.* Springfield, NJ: Enslow Publishers, Inc.

Sanford, W. R., & Green, C. R. (1997). *Sacagawea: Native American hero.* Springfield, NJ: Enslow Publishers, Inc.

Saunders, S. (1987). *Margaret Mead: The world was her family.* New York, NY: Viking Kestrel.

Savage, J. (1995). *Pioneering women of the wild west.* Springfield, NJ: Enslow Publishing, Inc.

Schwabacher, M. (1997). *Superstars of women's tennis.* Broomall, PA: Chelsea House Publishers.

Scott, E. (1995). *Adventure in space: The flight to fix the Hubble.* New York, NY: Hyperion.

Senn, J.A. (1993). *Jane Goodall.* Woodbridge, CT: Blackbuck Press.

Seymour, F. (1991). *Sacajawea: American pathfinder.* New York, NY: Macmillan.

Sheafer, S. A. (1996). *Women in America's wars.* Springfield, NJ: Enslow Publishers, Inc.

Sherrow, V. (1995). *Wilma Rudolph: Olympic champion.* Broomall, PA: Chelsea House Publishers.

Shore, N., & Horner, M. S. (1989). *Amelia Earhart: Aviator.* Broomall, PA: Chelsea House Publishers.

Siembieda, K., & Marciniszyn, A. (1989). *Adventures in the northern wilderness.* Taylor, MI: Palladium Books.

Smith, P., & Cohen, J. H. (1998). *Superstars of women's figure skating.* Broomall, PA: Chelsea House Publishers.

Sonneborn, L. (1991). *Clara Barton: American Red Cross founder.* Broomall, PA: Chelsea House Publishers.

Spence, J. (1995). *Julie Krone: Fearless jockey.* Vero Beach, FL: Rourke Publishing Group.

Spence, J. (1995). *Nancy Kerrigan: Courageous skater.* Vero Beach, FL: Rourke Publishing, Inc.

Stefoff, R. (1992). *Women of the world: Women travelers and explorers.* New York, NY: Oxford University Press.

Sternsker, B. (Ed.). (1990). *Women of valor.* Chicago, IL: Ivan Dee.

Stevens, B. (1984). *Deborah Sampson goes to war.* Minneapolis, MN: Carolrhoda Books.

Van Meter, V. (1995). *Taking flight: My story.* New York, NY: Viking.

Vare, E. A. (1992). *Adventurous spirit: A story about Ellen Swallow Richards.* Minneapolis, MN: Carolrhoda Books.

Wadsworth, G. (1994). *Susan Butcher: Sled dog racer.* Minneapolis, MN: Lerner Publishing Group.

Weisberg, B. (1990). *Susan B. Anthony: Woman suffragist.* Broomall, PA: Chelsea House Publishers.

Wellman, S. (1998). *Kristi Yamaguchi.* Broomall, PA: Chelsea House Publishers.

Wellman, S. (1998). *Mother Teresa: Missionary of charity.* Broomall, PA: Chelsea House Publishers.

Whitelaw, N. (1997). *Clara Barton: Civil War nurse.* Springfield, NJ: Enslow Publishers, Inc.

White, A. J. (1997). *Sacagawea.* Springfield, NJ: Enslow Publishers, Inc.

Wilner, B. (1997). *Superstars of women's golf.* Broomall, PA: Chelsea House Publishers.

Windle, J. (1994). *Adventures in South America.* Sisters, OR: Multnomah Publishers.

Wolf, S. (1994). *Focus: Five women photographers.* New York, NY: Albert Whitman.

Wood, L. H. (1996). *Amelia Earhart: Aviator.* Broomall, PA: Chelsea House Publishers.

Worth, R. (1999). *Women in combat.* Springfield, NJ: Enslow Publishers, Inc.

Wukovits, J. F. (1997). *Annie Oakley.* Broomall, PA: Chelsea House Publishers.

Ziesk, E., & Horner, M. S. (1990). *Margaret Mead.* New York: Chelsea House Publishers.

Books for Young Adults

Andrews, S. B., & Creed, J. (1998). *Authentic Alaska*. Lincoln, NB: University of Nebraska Press.

Boga, S. A. (1993). *Adventure athletes: Runners and walkers: Keeping pace with the world's best.* Harrisburg, PA: Stackpole.

Bougainville, L. A. (1990). *Adventure in the wilderness: The American journals of Louis Antoine de Bougainville, 1756-1760.* Norman, OK: University of Oklahoma Press.

Bowen, A. R. (1998). *Flying against the wind: A story about Beryl Markham.* Minneapolis, MN: Lerner Publishing Group.

Breitenbucher, C. (1994). *Bonnie Blair: Golden streak.* Minneapolis, MN: Lerner Publishing Group.

Briggs, C. S. (1999). *Women in space.* Minneapolis, MN: Lerner Publishing Group.

Brooks, P. (1990). *Beyond the myth: The story of Joan of Arc.* New York, NY: J.B. Lippincott.

Bryant, M. (1989). *Sacajawea: A Native American heroine*. Billings, MT: Council for Indian Education.

Chadwick, R. (1987). *Amelia Earhart: Aviation pioneer*. Minneapolis, MN: Lerner Publishing Group.

Coburn, B. (1997). *Everest*. New York, NY: Random House.

Cochran, J. (1954). *The stars at noon*. Boston, MA: Little, Brown and Company.

Dannett, S. (1959). *Noble women of the north*. New York, NY: Thomas Yoseloff.

De Rutte, T. (1992). *Adventures of a young Swiss in California: The gold rush account of Theophile de Rutte*. Sacramento, CA: Sacto Book Collectors.

Deschner, W. (1997). *Travels with a kayak*. Baker, OR: Eddie Tern Printing.

Donohue, S. (1993). *Kristi Yamaguchi: Artist on ice*. Minneapolis, MN: Lerner Publishing Group.

Earhart, A. (1977). *The fun of it*. Chicago, IL: Academy Press.

Earhart, A. (1979). *20 hours, 40 minutes*. Manchester, NH: Ayer Company Publishers, Inc.

Fehr, K. S. (1997). *Monica Seles: Returning champion*. Minneapolis, MN: Lerner Publishing Group.

Freeman L., & Bond, A. (1992). *America's first woman warrior.* New York, NY: Paragon House.

Galt, M. F. (1995). *Up to the plate: The all American girls professional baseball league.* Minneapolis, MN: Lerner Publishing Group.

Gatto, K. (1998). *Michelle Kwan: Champion on ice.* Minneapolis, MN: Lerner Publishing Group.

George, S. K. (1992). *Adventures of the woman homesteader: The life & letters of Elinore Pruitt Stewart.* Lincoln, NB: University of Nebraska Printing.

Gogol, S. (1998). *Katy Steding: Pro basketball pioneer.* Minneapolis, MN: Lerner Publishing Group.

Goldberg, V. (1987). *Margaret Bourke-White.* Reading, MA: Addison-Wesley.

Goldstein, M. J. (1993). *Jennifer Capriati: Tennis sensation.* Minneapolis, MN: Lerner Publishing Group.

Goldstein, M. J., & Larson, J. (1994). *Jackie Joyner-Kersee: Superwoman.* Minneapolis, MN: Lerner Publishing Group.

Goodall, J. (1990). *Through a window: My 30 years with the chimps of Gombe.* Boston, MA: Houghton Mifflin.

Hart, P. S. (1996). *Up in the air: The story of Bessie Coleman.* Minneapolis, MN: Lerner Publishing Group.

Hoehling, A. (1967). *Women who spied*. New York, NY: Dodd, Mead.

Howard, M. (1999). *Madeline Albright*. Minneapolis, MN: Lerner Publishing Group.

Howell, R. (Ed.). (1982). *Her story in sports: A historical anthology of women in sports*. West Point, NY: Leisure Press.

Hughes, M. (1998). *Juli Furtado: Rugged racer*. Minneapolis, MN: Lerner Publishing Group.

Jeneid, M. (1998). *Adventure kayaking: Trips from the Russian River to Monterey: Includes Lake Tahoe, Mono Lake, & Pyramid Lake*. Berkeley, CA: Wilderness Printing.

Keller, E. (1996). *Margaret Bourke-White: A photographer's life*. Minneapolis, MN: Lerner Publishing Group.

Keenan, S. (1996). *Scholastic encyclopedia of women in the United States*. New York, NY: Scholastic.

Kostmen, S. (1976). *Twentieth century women of achievement*. New York, NY: Richard Rosen Press.

Kroeger, B. (1994). *Nellie Bly: Daredevil, reporter, feminist*. New York, NY: Random House.

Kudlinski, K. (1991). *Helen Keller: A light for the blind*. New York, NY: Puffin Books.

Lauber, P. (1988). *Lost star: The story of Amelia Earhart*. New York, NY: Scholastic Inc.

Linnea, P. H., Houston, P., & Rogers, S. F., et al. (1998). *Gifts of the wild: A woman's book of adventure*: Seattle, WA: Printing Seal Feminist Publishing.

Lowery, L. (1996). *Wilma Mankiller.* Minneapolis, MN: Lerner Publishing Group.

Maxwell, J. (1997). *Femme d'adventure.* Seattle, WA: Seal Printing Feminist Publishing.

McMartin, B. & Brenning, L. M. (1996). *Adventures in camping: A young people's guide to Adirondack backpacking.* Utica, NY: North Country.

Miller, B. M. (1995). *Buffalo gals: Women of the old west.* Minneapolis, MN: Lerner Publishing Group.

Montgomery, S. (1991). *Walking with the great apes.* Boston, MA: Houghton Mifflin.

Moynihan, R. B., Armitage, S., & Dichamp, C. F. (1998). *So much to be done.* Lincoln, NB: Bison Books Corporation.

Olney, R. R. (1997). *Lyn St. James: Driven to be first.* Minneapolis, MN: Lerner Publishing Group.

Osland, J. S. (1995). *Adventure of working abroad: Hero tales from the global frontier.* San Francisco, CA: Jossey-Bass.

Reiter, J. S. (1978). *The women (the old west).* New York, NY: Time-Life Books.

Rovin, J. (1994). *Adventure heroes: Legendary characters from Odysseus to James Bond.* New York, NY: Facts on File.

Savage, J. (1996). *Julie Krone: Unstoppable jockey.* Minneapolis, MN: Lerner Publishing Group.

Schmidt, J. C. (1997). *Adventuring in the Rockies.* San Francisco, CA: Sierra Club.

Scott, E. (1998). *Adventure in space: The flight to fix the Hubble.* New York, NY: Hyperion Paperbacks.

Sheafer, S. A. (1978). *Gold rush women.* Sacramento, CA: Historical California Journal Publications.

Sierra Club Books Staff (1998). *Adventuring in the Alps.* New York, NY: Random House.

Ukens, L. L. (1997). *Adventure in the Amazon: Leader's guide.* San Francisco, CA: Jossey-Bass.

Wayne, S. (1991). *Adventuring in North Africa: The Sierra Club travel guide to Morocco, Algeria, Tunisia & the Maltese Islands.* San Francisco, CA: Sierra Club.

Welch, C. A. (1997). *Margaret Bourke-White.* Minneapolis, MN: Lerner Publishing Group.

Windle, J. (1994). *Adventures in South America.* Sisters, OR: Multnomah Publishing.

Zepatos, T. (1994). *Adventures in good company: The complete guide to women's tours and outdoor trips.* Portland, OR: Eighth Mount Printing.

Web Sites for
Women Adventurers

- **Role Models for the Future**
  http://4net.hr/crow/rolemode.htm

  > Gives information about numerous women who are or were leaders in adventurous fields such as traveling to the north pole, sailing solo around the world, etc.

- **Women's History Month**
  http://www.webrary.org/rs/bibwomen.html

  > Explores the role of women in American society including numerous adventurers.

- **Marathon Women**
  www.comrads.com/pr008.htm

  > Lists some women who are extraordinary athletes.

- **Women in the Gold Rush**
  www.gold-rush.org/ALASKA/stories/Ala03r.html

- **American Women in History**
  www.usgennet.org/~alhnazus/ women.html

  Assorted listing for web pages about historical women figures.

- **Notable Women Ancestors-Adventurers**
  www.rootsweb.com/ ~nwa/adventurer.html

  Gives information about women adventurers.

About the Authors

Dr. Frances A. Karnes is Professor of Special Education and for the past 20 years has served as Director of the Frances A. Karnes Center for Gifted Studies at The University of Southern Mississippi, where she has been a member of the faculty since being awarded the doctorate by the University of Illinois in 1973. For the past 16 years, she has also served as Director of the Leadership Studies Program at USM. She has become widely known for her research, publications, innovative program developments, and service activities in gifted education, leadership training, legal issues, and girls. Among the 15 books and more than 180 journal articles that bear her name as author and co-author are four books focusing on girls and young women.

Dr. Karnes' rich background of experience in leadership roles at local, state, and national levels includes service as president of two state professional societies and a major national organization, The Association for the Gifted. Currently, she serves on the editorial boards of several professional journals and is a member of the Board of Directors of the National Association for Gifted Children, the Operational Volunteer Board of the Girl Scouts of the United States of America, and the Board of Trustees of Quincy University.

Dr. Suzanne M. Bean is a Professor of Education at Mississippi University for Women (MUW). For the past 20 years, she has served in the field of Gifted Studies as a teacher of gifted students, Director of the Mississippi Governor's School, founder and Director of various other pro- grams for gifted students, their teachers, and their parents. She is currently serving as Coordinator of Gifted Youth Programs and Graduate Programs in Gifted Studies and Instructional Management at MUW.

Dr. Bean has co-authored four books for young adults, and has had numerous publications in professional journals. She serves on the Editorial Review Board for *Gifted Child Quarterly* and *The Journal for Secondary Gifted Education*. She has been President of the Mississippi Association for Talented and Gifted, and is currently serving as a delegate to the Executive Board of the National Conference on Governor's Schools. For the past two decades, she has made numerous pre- sentations at the state, regional, and national levels. In 1997/1998, Dr. Bean was selected by MUW students as Faculty Member of the Year.